Bureau of Justice Assistance

A Policymaker's Guide to Hate Crimes

March 1997
Reprinted November 1999

Monograph

NCJ 162304

Foreword

In recent years hate crimes and related legal issues have received a significant amount of coverage and commentary in the news media. As a result of several dramatic incidents of hate crimes and domestic terrorism, public awareness and concern over bias-motivated crimes have heightened, and the topic has steadily moved up the political agendas of leaders at every level of government. These developments have led Attorney General Janet Reno to seek an assessment of laws and strategies designed to fight, gauge, and prevent bias-motivated offenses; this monograph both reflects and helps meet that commitment.

A Policymaker's Guide to Hate Crimes is the product of a review of recent literature on hate crimes, interviews with hate crime experts, and attendance at congressional hearings and a planning meeting on hate crimes and terrorism. It is meant to explain, in layperson's terms, the scope and nature of the Nation's hate crime problem and to provide a general overview of the current responses to hate crimes by local, State, and Federal government agencies; law enforcement authorities; and civil rights groups.

This monograph examines the significant strides made by the Federal Government in creating a baseline of raw data on hate crimes and the problems that impede the reporting of hate crime incidents. In addition, the monograph summarizes current State laws and U.S. Supreme Court decisions regarding hate crimes. Preventive measures and tactics for dealing with hate crime offenders also are discussed with references to vanguard programs in specific communities.

We hope that this monograph will educate and guide public officials in developing policies that address one of the Nation's most insidious problems.

Nancy E. Gist
Director

Acknowledgments

The Bureau of Justice Assistance (BJA) would like to acknowledge the following National Criminal Justice Association staff members for their contributions as authors of this monograph: Gwen Holden, former Executive Vice President, Paul E. Lawrence, Director of Administration and Information Systems, Lisa Doyle Moran, Associate Director for Legal Affairs, Robert Kapler, Senior Staff Associate and Project Leader, and Jennifer A. Ferrante, former Staff Attorney.

BJA would also like to acknowledge the assistance provided by Michael Lieberman, Associate Director/Counsel, D.C. Office, the Anti-Defamation League; Brian Levin, former Counsel, Klanwatch, Southern Poverty Law Center; Jack McDevitt, Co-Director, Center for Criminal Justice Policy Research, College of Criminal Justice, Northeastern University (Massachusetts); Helen Gonzales, Public Policy Director, National Gay and Lesbian Task Force and Policy Institute; Daniel Katz, Legislative Counsel, American Civil Liberties Union; Darryl Borgquist, Media Affairs Officer, U.S. Department of Justice's Community Relations Service; the staff of the U.S. Department of Justice, Federal Bureau of Investigation's Uniform Crime Report Program; and the staff of the U.S. Department of Justice's National Criminal Justice Reference Service.

BJA would like to thank Faith Mitchell, Rosemary Chalk, and Janine Bilyeu, National Research Council, Commission on Behavioral and Social Sciences and Education, Committee on Law and Justice, who made it possible for the authors of this monograph to take part in a seminal planning meeting on hate crimes and terrorism.

BJA appreciates the assistance of the National Crime Prevention Council (NCPC), which allowed BJA to use information from the bias crime section of the NCPC book *350 Tested Strategies To Prevent Crime: A Resource for Municipal Agencies and Community Groups* (Washington, D.C., 1995). The information from that book became an integral part of the monograph chapter on specific hate-crime-related responses and initiatives.

Table of Contents

Table of Contents (continued)

Executive Summary

Despite the best efforts of political and community leaders to foster tolerance and understanding, deep-seated racial tensions continue to plague the Nation. News stories of bias-motivated incidents fill the national pages of major U.S. newspapers. A rash of arsons at African-American churches in the South, for example, has spurred the Federal Government to launch a major investigation that, so far, has led to the arrest of 120 suspects. Of the 298 Federal arson investigations carried out between January 1995 and November 1996, approximately 43 percent involved fires at black churches, although white churches far outnumber black churches in the Nation. Political and religious leaders said that the disproportionate number of black churches being burned indicated that the Nation was experiencing a serious wave of hate crimes.

Hate Crime History

While the hate crime problem has moved up the political agendas of policymakers at every level of government in recent years, the phenomenon is hardly new.

From the Romans' persecution of Christians and the Nazis' —final solution" for the Jews to the —ethnic cleansing" in Bosnia and genocide in Rwanda, hate crimes have shaped and sometimes defined world history. In the United States, racial and religious biases largely have inspired most hate crimes. As Europeans began to colonize the New World in the 16th and 17th centuries, Native Americans increasingly became the targets of bias-motivated intimidation and violence. During the past two centuries, some of the more typical examples of hate crimes in this Nation include the lynchings of African Americans, cross burnings to drive black families from predominantly white neighborhoods, assaults on homosexuals, and the painting of swastikas on Jewish synagogues.

What Is a Hate Crime?

For the purposes of this monograph, hate crimes, or bias-motivated crimes, are defined as offenses motivated by hatred against a victim based on his or her race, religion, sexual orientation, handicap, ethnicity, or national origin. While such a definition may make identifying a hate crime seem like a simple task, criminal acts motivated by bias can easily be confused with forms of expression protected by the U.S. Constitution.

What Makes Hate Crimes Different From Other Crimes?

The number of hate crimes may seem small when compared with the incidence of other types of crimes in the United States. In 1993, for example, 11 of the 24,526 murders reported in the United States were classified as hate crimes, as were 13 of the 104,806 reported rapes. But the simple truth about hate crimes is that each offense victimizes not one victim but many. A hate crime victimizes not only the immediate target but every member of the group that the immediate target represents. A bias-motivated offense can cause a broad ripple of discomfiture among members of a targeted group, and a violent hate crime can act like a virus, quickly spreading feelings of terror and loathing across an entire community. Apart from their psychological impacts, violent hate crimes can create tides of retaliation and counterretaliation. Therefore, criminal acts motivated by bias may carry far more weight than other types of criminal acts.

Causes and Characteristics of Hate Crimes

A host of factors may create a climate in which people, motivated by their biases, take criminal action. Such factors include poor or uncertain economic conditions, racial stereotypes in films and on television, hate-filled discourse on talk shows or in political advertisements, the use of racial code language such as —welfare mothers" and —inner city thugs," and an individual's personal experiences with members of particular minority groups. Once a climate of hate is created, a single incident—such as the videotaped beating of Los Angeles, California, motorist Rodney King—can trigger a wave of hate crimes.

Hate Crime Victims

African Americans, who constitute the single largest minority group in the Nation, are more likely to be targets of hate crimes than members of any other group. Of the nearly 8,000 hate crimes reported in 1995, almost 3,000 of them were motivated by bias against African Americans. Other typical victims are Jews, homosexuals, Muslims, and, increasingly, Asian Americans.

Hate Crime Perpetrators

Most hate crimes are committed not by members of an organized hate group but by individual citizens. Some perpetrators resent the growing economic power of a particular racial or ethnic group and engage in —scapegoating"; others react to a perceived threat to the safety and property value of their neighborhood. Still other offenders include —thrill seekers"—those who randomly target interchangeable representatives of minority groups for harassment and violence, and —mission offenders"—

those who believe they are on a mission to rid the world of some perceived evil. This last group accounts for a tiny percentage of bias-motivated offenders. The majority of offenders—and passive observers—are merely individuals who believe racial and ethnic stereotypes and act on spur-of-the-moment impulses. Frequently alcohol or drug use is a factor in the commission of hate crimes.

Are Hate Crimes Increasing?

Data Collection

The Hate Crime Statistics Act of 1990 (HCSA) directs the U.S. Attorney General to collect data from State and local law enforcement agencies about crimes that —manifest evidence of prejudice based upon race, religion, sexual orientation, or ethnicity." Submission of such data is voluntary. The Federal Bureau of Investigation's (FBI) Uniform Crime Report (UCR) Program is the Nation's central repository of hate crime statistics.

When the UCR issued its first report on hate crimes in January 1993, fewer than one in five of the Nation's law enforcement agencies were providing data on these crimes. As of October 1996, nearly 60 percent of the 16,000 law enforcement agencies that participated in the UCR were contributing hate crime data, and 19 States had enacted statutes that mandated hate crime data collection. More agencies are expected to provide data on hate crimes as States convert to the National Incident Based Reporting System (NIBRS), a new, more comprehensive crime reporting system that collects a variety of crime information, including whether a crime was motivated by bias and the demographic characteristics of both the victim and offender.

Hate Crime Trends

While there has been a concerted effort to establish a statistical baseline of hate crimes at the national level, uncertainty still exists about whether the —hate crime rate" is rising or falling. Nationally, the volume of hate crime incidents *seems* to have increased dramatically in 1992, stabilized and dipped during the following 2 years, then increased again in 1995. According to the FBI, State and local law enforcement agencies in 1991 reported 4,755 bias-motivated crimes, including 12 murders. The number of reported hate crimes rose to 7,466 incidents in 1992 and to 7,587 incidents in 1993. Reported hate crimes dropped nearly 30 percent to 5,852 incidents in 1994, then increased in 1995 to 7,947 incidents, including 20 murders (see figure A on page 7).

However, because many agencies do not submit hate crime data or have not recorded hate crime incidents, these statistics are suspect. If the number of incidents reported each year is compared with the number of agencies reporting, quite a different story emerges. The ratio of the number of incidents per reporting agency peaked in 1991 and has been on a downward slide ever since, with a slight bump up in 1995 (see figure B on page 7).

As of October 1996, five States still did not collect hate crime data. Yet even if all States were reporting these incidents it would be difficult to gauge the level of the hate crime problem in this country because bias-motivated crimes typically are underreported by both law enforcement agencies *and* victims.

Disparities in Statistics

Since the first UCR on hate crimes was released for 1991, hate crime data from law enforcement agencies have differed significantly from those compiled by private organizations. One of the reasons for the disparity is that, while law enforcement agencies report only actual crimes, advocacy groups usually report all —incidents," even those that may not rise to the level of a criminal offense. Many police jurisdictions, especially those in rural areas, simply do not have the manpower, inclination, or technical expertise to record hate crimes, and other jurisdictions fear that admitting the existence of hate crimes will cause their communities cultural, political, and economic repercussions. Some private organizations, on the other hand, record *all* hate crime incidents, even unconfirmed reports from anonymous sources.

Why Some Victims Fail To Report Hate Crimes

Victims have a myriad of reasons for failing to report hate crimes. Homosexual victims may decide not to report hate crimes to police because of fears of reprisals or a belief that they will be forced —out of the closet." Such an —oting" may cause repercussions to their career and relationships with family and friends. Some victims have little confidence that authorities will bring the perpetrators to justice. Immigrant hate crime victims may not be proficient in English or may be undocumented aliens who fear that any contact with police will increase their risk of deportation. Other immigrants come from cultures that mistrust law enforcement agencies, or they believe that victims of bias-motivated crime are somehow stigmatized. Some victims refuse to report such crimes because they want to avoid the humiliation of recounting the event.

What Has Been Done To Combat Hate Crimes?

To prevent future tides of hate crimes, political leaders, law enforcement agencies, State and Federal agencies, and public interest groups have been working together to identify and track hate crimes and to mitigate the conditions that foster them.

Hate Crimes and the Law

Forty-seven jurisdictions across the United States have enacted some form of legislation designed to combat hate crimes. Thirty-nine States have enacted laws against bias-motivated violence and intimidation. Nineteen States have statutes that specifically mandate the collection of hate crime data. Meanwhile, dozens of law enforcement agencies have promulgated new policies and procedures to address hate crimes.

In two recent U.S. Supreme Court decisions, the Court upheld a hate crime penalty-enhancement statute but struck down an ordinance that criminalized —ighting words" uttered to provoke violence against individuals because of their —race çolor, creed, religion, or gender."

Hate Crime Initiatives

In the past 4 years, Congress and the Justice Department have approved several new initiatives designed to combat hate crimes and violence. Several of these initiatives were included in the 1992 reauthorization of the Juvenile Justice and Delinquency Prevention Act, as amended. Among the measures was a requirement that each State's juvenile delinquency prevention plan include a component designed to combat hate crimes. Another requirement was that the Justice Department's Office of Juvenile Justice and Delinquency Prevention (OJJDP) conduct a national assessment of young persons who commit hate crimes.

The Justice Department's Community Relations Service (CRS), the only Federal agency that exists primarily to assist communities in addressing intergroup disputes, has played a unique role in helping to identify and prevent hate crimes. CRS has participated in HCSA training sessions for hundreds of law enforcement officials from dozens of police agencies across the Nation and has assisted schools and school districts in addressing racial tension and conflict through programs in peer mediation.

The newest and most innovative response to bias-motivated crimes is the formation of —hate crime response networks," which serve as information clearinghouses on rights and services. Massachusetts, California, and a few other States are working to set up such networks. The California Association of Official Human Relations Agencies, for example, is developing regional hate violence response networks in 10 regions in the State. The network is set up like a wheel with many spokes. At the hub is a human rights commission or other appropriate public agency or nonprofit organization that designates staff to coordinate the project or acts as a fiscal agent. A series of committees make up the —spokes," each representing a different focus area, such as community activities, criminal justice, schools, the media, and youth.

The Anti-Defamation League (ADL) has been involved in a number of youth intervention and hate crime education programs. In Massachusetts, for example, ADL staffers from the organization's Boston regional office and the A World of Difference Institute worked with the State Attorney General's Office to develop the Youth Diversion Project, in which nonviolent youth offenders are diverted into alternative education and community service programs.

The Southern Poverty Law Center has a track record of bringing lawsuits against organizations whose members commit hate crimes on their behalf. In two recent cases, the center won judgments of $12.5 million and $7 million, respectively, against the White Aryan Resistance and the Ku Klux Klan for the deaths by beating and lynching of two African-American men. The center recently filed suit against a State Ku Klux Klan organization on behalf of an African-American church that was torched by a Klan member.

Hate crime response experts—including representatives from the ADL—are helping to develop a model curriculum for the Federal Law Enforcement Training Center to be used in the instruction of Federal, State, and local police officials. The National Gay and Lesbian Task Force (NGLTF), meanwhile, has provided staff support, literature, and technical assistance to community anti-violence projects as well as local gay and lesbian groups. The NGLTF also lobbies to have sexual orientation included in the lists of protected groups in State statutes and local ordinances. Beyond its routine support activities, the NGLTF intervenes in individual cases, keeps files on political candidates, and publishes a —scre card" that rates a candidate's support or opposition to gay and lesbian rights issues.

Increasingly, religious groups are recognizing the need to promote racial and cultural tolerance. One example is the Racial Reconciliation Initiative, sponsored by the National Black Evangelical Association and the National Association of Evangelicals. Under the initiative, materials are disseminated that help Christians understand the source of conflicts between races.

What More Can Policymakers Do?

When law enforcement officers are trained to identify, respond to, and record hate crime incidents, more hate crimes actually are reported, responded to, and prosecuted. The investigation, prosecution, and punishment of especially notorious or high-profile hate crimes tends to promote even more reporting by victims and witnesses. If potential victims know a reporting system is in place and see a well-publicized case result in a stiff sentence for the perpetrators, they will be more likely to report a hate crime in the future and would-be perpetrators will be discouraged from acting on their impulses. Thus policymakers may want to focus on developing initiatives and strategies that promote training for law enforcement officers, prosecutors, and judges and new laws to ensure that all hate crimes are recorded and acted upon.

Actions for Policymakers To Consider

Following is a list of focus areas that policymakers might want to consider to enhance hate crime responses by law enforcement agencies and to help reduce the number of bias-motivated incidents:

◊ Despite the problems inherent in collecting hate crime statistics on a national level, hate crime experts agree that the Federal Government is headed in the right direction by accumulating and disseminating these data. Policymakers might want to consider ways to provide a permanent mandate for the HCSA to ensure that hate crime data remain a fixed part of the UCR and possibly are reported in the same document as other crime statistics.

◊ Recognizing the importance of collecting accurate data on hate crimes, State policymakers might want to support or introduce legislation that mandates such data collection by all law enforcement agencies in the State as part of their regular UCR reporting process. In States without data collection laws, policymakers might want to support or sponsor legislation that requires law enforcement agencies to collect hate crime data.

◊ Law enforcement personnel must be able to identify, record, and act on hate crimes in an effective, timely manner. Policymakers at the State and Federal levels might want to make hate crime training a regular part of all law enforcement training. The Administration and Congress may want to take measures to ensure that the FBI continues to offer hate crime training and education to new and veteran field agents. The FBI also may want to obtain sufficient funding to continue to respond to requests for hate crime training from State and local law enforcement agencies.

◊ Accurately reporting and properly investigating and prosecuting hate crimes takes thorough and systematic training. Policymakers at both the State and Federal levels might want to pass legislation that provides funding incentives to State and local law enforcement agencies to help support such training.

◊ There are widespread disparities between the hate crime data provided by government agencies and the data provided by public interest groups. Political leaders might want to bring representatives of law enforcement agencies and private groups —to the table" to develop and agree on a standard definition and reporting protocol for hate crimes.

◊ The newest and most innovative response to bias-motivated crimes is the formation of —hate crime response networks," which serve as information clearinghouses. Policymakers at the State and Federal levels might want to support or sponsor legislation to provide funding for State and local hate crime response networks.

◊ Part of becoming a good citizen means learning to understand other races and cultures. State and local policymakers may want to ensure that hate crime awareness or ethnic diversity curriculums are provided in both elementary and secondary schools. Such a curriculum recently was developed by Educational Development Center Inc. under a grant from OJJDP.

Origins and Definition of Hate Crimes

Hate Crimes Then and Now

The problem of hate crimes is hardly a recent phenomenon. Earliest recorded history to the present is rife with accounts of individuals committing acts of intimidation and barbaric violence against others simply because of their race, religion, physical handicap, sex, or political beliefs. From the Romans' persecution of Christians to the Nazis' "final solution" for the Jews, from the "ethnic cleansing" in Bosnia to the genocide in Rwanda, hate crimes have shaped and sometimes defined the history of nations.[1]

In the United States, hate crimes have been inspired largely by racial and religious biases. As Europeans began to colonize the New World in the 16th and 17th centuries, Native Americans increasingly became the targets of bias-motivated intimidation and violence. During the past two centuries, the Ku Klux Klan's lynchings of African Americans, cross burnings to drive black families from predominantly white neighborhoods, and swastikas painted on Jewish synagogues are some of the more typical examples of hate crimes in this Nation.

Since the mid-1980's, the problem of hate crimes in the United States has received mounting public scrutiny, largely as a result of several sensational incidents. The shooting death of controversial radio talk show host Alan Berg in Denver, Colorado, in 1984 focused national attention on the activities of a heretofore unknown cadre of white supremacists. Two years later, three African-American men were attacked—one fatally—after their car broke down in a white New York City neighborhood called Howard Beach. The news coverage and analysis that followed these incidents heightened public awareness of hate crimes and moved the problem up the political agenda at both the State and national levels.[2]

As a subject for news stories, hate crimes have gained increasing prominence during the past decade. A check of the Nexis™ computer database for selected years illustrates the ascendancy of "hate crimes" in the public's consciousness. Searching for stories containing the terms "hate crimes," "bias-motivated crimes," or "gay-bashing" turned up 14 entries for 1986; 88 entries for 1988; 572 entries for 1990; 1,207 entries for 1992; 1,215 entries for 1994; and 1,021 entries for 1995. The 364 "hits" for 1996 as of April 10, 1996, include the following incidents:

0   In North Carolina three soldiers from Fort Bragg were charged in the racially motivated killing of an African-American couple in Fayetteville

in December 1995. The incident led to an Army investigation in March 1996 into the involvement of U.S. soldiers in extremist and hate groups.

0 Three predominantly African-American churches were burned in Louisiana in February 1996, and four churches had been burned in Alabama since December 22, 1995.

0 Also in February 1996, Virginia State police were asked to help local police investigate attacks on area houses of worship. The vandalizing of two Jewish synagogues brought the number of religious facilities that had been attacked in the State in recent months to four.

0 Police in St. Alban, Vermont, arrested two teens in a racially motivated beating in February 1996 that left a 19-year-old Hispanic man blind in one eye. A pipe, a tree limb, and a broken hockey stick apparently were used in the attack, police said.

0 In March 1996 in Corvallis, Oregon, racial epithets were scrawled on several posters depicting African Americans on the campus of Oregon State University, which is trying to increase minority enrollment. An African-American student also reported that three students on a dormitory roof shouted racial slurs at him in March 1996.

0 In Mamaroneck, New York, a $15,000 reward was offered for the arrest of vandals who spray painted hate messages on seven houses in February 1996; six of the homes belonged to Jewish families.

Defining Hate Crimes

While —hate crime" would be the term most often used in the United States to describe an attack by a white supremacist against an African American, the act would be known in Germany as —right-wing violence" or —xeno-phobic violence." In Britain and France, it would be referred to simply as —racial violence."[3]

The term —hate crime" entered the lexicon most likely because it is broad enough to cover offenses perpetrated not only against African Americans, but also against gays, Muslims, Koreans, and members of various other groups. The Hate Crime Statistics Act of 1990 (see Chapter 1) defines hate crimes as —crimes that manifest evidence of prejudice based on race, religion, sexual orientation, or ethnicity, including where appropriate the crimes of murder, non-negligent manslaughter, forcible rape, aggravated assault, simple assault, intimidation, arson, and destruction, damage or vandalism of property."

By 1993, fewer than half the States had adopted the Federal definition of a hate crime, while other States had added other victim categories. Connecticut, for example, adds people with physical disabilities to the list of possible victims; Illinois' definition includes —color, creed, ancestry, and physical and mental disability"; and Rhode Island's definition includes disability and gender. On the other hand, Pennsylvania does not recognize sexual orientation as a victim classification.[4]

For the purposes of this report, hate crimes—or bias-motivated crimes—are defined as offenses motivated by hatred against a victim based on his or her race, religion, sexual orientation, ethnicity, or national origin.

While such a definition may make identifying a hate crime seem like a simple task, criminal acts motivated by bias can easily be confused with forms of expression protected by the U.S. Constitution. A person's biases may compel him to announce his dislike for the practice of homosexuality, which would not rise to the level of a hate crime, or may spur him to smear a swastika on a building or commit homicide, which most certainly would be identified as hate crimes.

Scope of the Hate Crimes Problem

Introduction

In the area of criminal justice, it is a political reality that public policy sometimes is driven more by emotions and perceptions—sometimes misperceptions—than hard empirical data. Still, any State or local official who is attempting to fashion sound public policy relating to hate crimes must rely on statistics at one time or another. Whether the best evidence shows that the number of bias-motivated offenses is increasing or waning in a geographic area will determine, to some extent, the level of resources that a policymaker will want to expend to solve a hate crime problem.

To that end, various social organizations, Congress, and the U.S. Department of Justice have made significant strides in recent years toward establishing a statistical "baseline" of hate crimes.

Hate Crime Statistics Act

In response to a perceived increase in hate crimes in the late 1980's, especially skinhead attacks on racial minorities, Congress in 1990 passed legislation setting up a Federal system for keeping track of bias-motivated incidents.[5]

The legislation, originally sponsored by Rep. John Conyers (D–Michigan) and Sen. Paul Simon (D–Illinois), was signed into law in April 1990 as the Hate Crime Statistics Act (HCSA) (codified at 28 U.S.C. 534). The act directs the U.S. Attorney General to acquire and publish annual data about crimes that "manifest evidence of prejudice based upon race, religion, sexual orientation, or ethnicity." Such data are to be collected from State and local law enforcement agencies, although submission is voluntary. In an effort to help law enforcement agencies to identify hate crimes accurately, the act also requires the Attorney General to establish guidelines for the collection of such data.

The offenses covered by the act are homicide; non-negligent manslaughter; forcible rape; assault; intimidation; arson; and destruction, damage, or vandalism of property.

Since passage of the act, the FBI has served as the central repository of bias-motivated crime statistics. The FBI's Hate Crime Data Collection Program, a component of the agency's Uniform Crime Report (UCR) Program, is managed by the agency's Criminal Justice Information Services Division. When HCSA expired on December 31, 1994, FBI Director Louis Freeh ordered that hate crime data collection continue.[6]

As of March 1996, the UCR had conducted 61 training conferences nation-wide. A total of nearly 3,700 conference attendees came from the 50 States and the District of Columbia and represented 1,199 separate law enforcement agencies.[7]

To assist the FBI in its training efforts, the Justice Department's Office for Victims of Crime (OVC) funded a project to develop a comprehensive hate crime training curriculum. The curriculum and training manual, prepared by the Massachusetts-based Education Development Center Inc. and the Massachusetts Criminal Justice Training Council, were released as the —National Bias Crimes Training for Law Enforcement and Victim Assistance Professionals."

The FBI intends to study reporting differences among law enforcement agencies with the Criminal Justice Policy Research Institute at Northeastern University, Boston, Massachusetts. The FBI also intends to begin collecting data on disability bias crime.[8]

When the UCR issued its first report on hate crimes statistics for January 1991, 2,771 agencies in 32 States submitted data—fewer than 1 in 5 of the Nation's law enforcement agencies. Many localities were unable or unwilling to collect data because of tight budgets and limited manpower.[9] In 1992, 6,181 law enforcement agencies in 41 States and the District of Columbia—an increase of 3,410 agencies—participated in the program. As of October 1996, nearly 60 percent of the 16,000 law enforcement agencies that participate in the UCR were contributing hate crime data, and 19 States had enacted statutes that mandated hate crime data collection.

Because hate crimes are not defined as separate, distinct offenses but are traditional crimes motivated by a particular bias, hate crime reporting is complicated by the need to determine offender motivation. In 1990 the FBI consolidated the Hate Crime Data Collection Program within both the existing UCR summary program and the National Incident Based Reporting System (NIBRS). NIBRS is a new, more comprehensive crime reporting system that collects a variety of crime information, including whether a crime was motivated by bias and the demographic characteristics of both victim and offender. Bias motivation for a crime is one of the 56 facts collected for each offense record under the new crime reporting format. More agencies are expected to provide data on hate crimes as States convert to the NIBRS. As of March 1996, 10 States had converted from summary UCR reporting to NIBRS.[10] As of March another 21 State agencies and 3 Federal agencies[11] had submitted test data to the NIBRS, and 12 other State agencies, the District of Columbia, and Guam were in various stages of planning and development to convert to NIBRS.

Hate Crime Trends

While there has been a concerted effort to establish a statistical baseline of hate crimes at the national level, uncertainty still exists about whether the

—hate crime rate" is rising or falling. —The bottom line is that we don't know. It looks as if the best data we have is incomplete,"[12] said Jack McDevitt, co-author of *Hate Crimes: The Rising Tide of Bigotry and Bloodshed.*[13]

Nationally, the volume of hate crime incidents *seems* to have increased dramatically in 1992, stabilized and dipped during the following 2 years, then increased again in 1995 (see figure A below). However, if the number of incidents reported each year is compared with the number of agencies reporting, quite a different story emerges. The ratio of the number of incidents per reporting agency peaked in 1991 and has been on a downward slide ever since, with a slight bump up in 1995 (see figure B below).

Figure A.   Hate Crimes: Agencies Reporting and Total Incidents

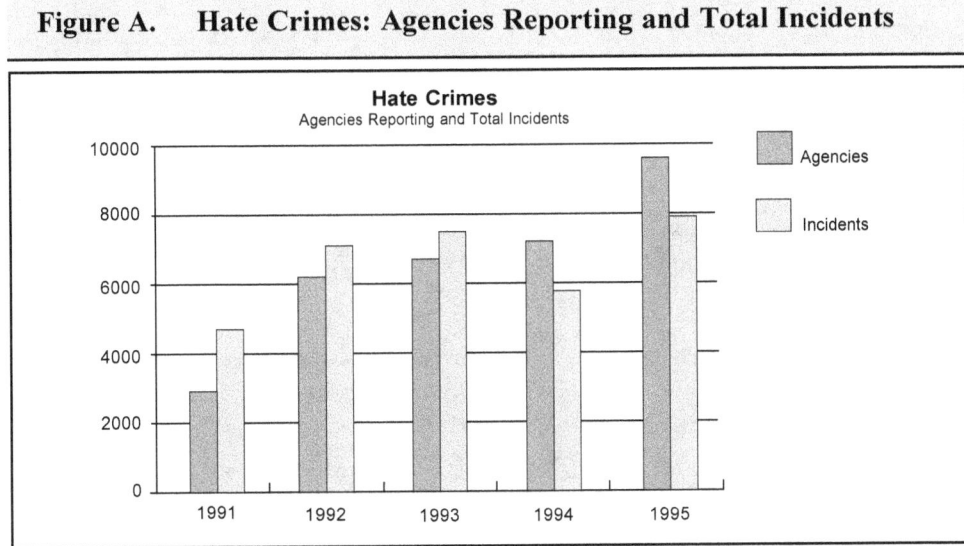

Figure B.   Hate Crimes: Average Incidents per Agency

According to the FBI, State and local law enforcement agencies in 1991 reported 4,755 bias-motivated crimes, including 12 murders. The number of reported hate crimes rose to 7,466 incidents in 1992 and to 7,587 incidents in 1993. Reported hate crimes dropped nearly 30 percent to 5,852 incidents in 1994, then increased in 1995 to 7,947 incidents, including 20 murders.[14]

As of October 1996, five States still did not collect hate crime data. Yet even if all States were reporting these incidents, it would be difficult to gauge the true extent of the hate crime problem in this country because bias-motivated crimes typically are underreported by both law enforcement agencies *and* victims.[15]

Disparities in Statistics

Since the first FBI hate crime report was released, there has continued to be a wide disparity between figures supplied by law enforcement agencies and those compiled by various private organizations.

The first FBI report, for instance, showed that 421 hate crimes were committed nationwide against homosexuals in 1991. Meanwhile, the National Gay and Lesbian Task Force (NGLTF) Policy Institute listed 1,822 such incidents in 5 major urban areas alone in 1991: Boston, Chicago, New York, San Francisco, and Minneapolis/St. Paul.[16]

The UCR for 1994 reported 677 antihomosexual incidents in the Nation, down from the 860 incidents reported the previous year. According to a report for 1994 released by the New York City Gay and Lesbian Anti-Violence Project, for *each* incident classified as antihomosexual by local law enforcement, *4.67 incidents* were classified as antihomosexual by community agencies.[17]

For 1994, the Anti-Defamation League (ADL) documented a total of 2,066 incidents of anti-Semitic harassment, violence, and vandalism—the highest in the ADL's *Audit of Anti-Semitic Incidents*' 16-year history. The FBI, however, reported 908 anti-Semitic incidents for that year—less than half the ADL's figure.

The UCR reported 258 hate crime incidents involving Asian and Pacific Islander Americans in 1993 and 209 incidents in 1994, a decrease of 18 percent. However, the National Asian Pacific American Legal Consortium reported 452 incidents of violent hate crimes against Asian and Pacific Islander Americans in 1994, a 35-percent increase from the number the group reported the previous year in its first annual report.[18]

A drop of nearly one-third in the number of officially reported incidents in 1994—despite the fact that 6 percent more agencies had recorded hate crimes incidents than the previous year—generated a fair amount of skepticism among public interest groups over the reliability of the UCR data. Some jurisdictions were suspected of trying to ignore or cover up very real hate crime problems.

"There's a disconnect in the FBI's 1994 hate crime statistics," said David H. Strassler, ADL national chairman, and Abraham H. Foxman, ADL national director, in a joint statement released by the ADL in February 1996.

Despite the disparities, public interest groups consider the establishment of a national baseline of statistics essential. "The ADL considers a two-paragraph box in *USA Today* that shows the numbers are declining a bad thing," said Michael Leiberman, associate director/counsel of the ADL's Washington, D.C., office. "When the numbers are up, [it] . . . means that at least the problem is being addressed."[19]

Said NGLTF's Helen Gonzales, "You can read the statistics in a couple of ways. More law enforcement agencies reporting means that more officers are becoming sensitized to the issue of hate crimes. Secondly, even if statistics show a dip in [hate crime incidents], they are a reflection that a problem still exists out there. Sure, we would love for there to be better collection by law enforcement agencies in the States. But this is a start."[20]

Factors Influencing Reporting

For various reasons many victims do not report hate crimes, and public service organizations and police agencies report hate crimes differently.

Depending on the jurisdiction, local law enforcement may only record and report bias-motivated "crimes"—those incidents that have been reported, investigated, and categorized as hate crimes. Some advocacy groups, on the other hand, classify all bias-motivated "incidents" as hate crimes, whether or not they rise to the level of criminal offense.[21]

The FBI prescribes a two-tiered decisionmaking process to determine whether a perpetrator was motivated by bias. An officer must follow a rigorous protocol that involves answering the following questions:

0 Is the motive of the perpetrator known to be bias?

0 Does the victim perceive a bias?

0 Are there any other reasons for the incident?

0 Did the incident occur on or near a religious holiday?

0 Are there relevant demographic factors that might create resentment or bias?

0 Are there any symbols involved in the incident that are associated with hate groups (such as Nazi swastikas)?

Once those questions are answered, a second review takes place in the police department before the crime is classified as a hate crime.[22]

Some law enforcement agencies have a looser definition of "hate crimes," while other jurisdictions, especially those in rural areas, simply do not have the manpower, inclination, and technical expertise to record hate crime incidents separately.[23]

Given the incendiary nature of hate crimes, some State and local political leaders and law enforcement officials discourage police and sheriff's departments from collecting or disseminating raw data. They consider any evidence of hate crimes a "black eye" on their community and fear the possible economic and political repercussions. [24]

"It's alarming that a number of communities reporting said that no hate crimes were committed within their jurisdictions," said Stephen Arent, vice chairman of the ADL's National Civil Rights Committee. "Unfortunately there is a great deal of denial. Many communities would say that hate crimes don't exist."[25]

Public interest organizations have developed their own methods and protocols for reporting hate crime incidents, and as a result their numbers rarely match Federal statistics. Some organizations diligently record all incidents—including bias-motivated comments—as hate crimes and accept reports from all sources, even anonymous sources.[26]

Many victims refuse to report hate crime incidents. Some victims believe they would be revictimized, especially if they come into periodic contact with the offender(s). Homosexuals often are reluctant to report an incident because they might be forced "out of the closet" and would suffer repercussions to their career and relationships with family and friends from such an "outing."[27]

Some victims do report incidents but to no avail. "In many cases, victims of anti-gay violence have reported the incident to the police and either have not been taken seriously or the incident was not pursued as a hate crime. I've been working in my job only 6 months, and the [anti-gay] violence has predominated everything I do," said Gonzales.[28]

While the problem of victim underreporting is particularly significant in the gay and lesbian community, the stigma of "coming out" has lessened in recent years. High-profile declarations by entertainment, sports, and political figures such as k.d. lang, Elton John, Martina Navratilova, and Rep. Barney Frank (D–Massachusetts), point toward a growing acceptance and tolerance of the gay lifestyle. The reality, however, still is quite different, Gonzales said. Recent incidents of violence against gays in Colorado, Oregon, and Maine, among other States, underscore the assertion that, in many areas, gays "have the appearance of equality but not the fact of equality."[29]

"In certain communities, especially urban communities such as Washington, D.C., and San Francisco, people do feel more comfortable coming out" than they would have felt a few years ago, Gonzales said. "As you move to rural areas and the center of the country, the comfort level with coming out is not as great, and those are the areas where gays and lesbians will be less likely to report hate crimes."[30]

Immigrants who become hate crime victims may have difficulty speaking English or may be undocumented aliens who fear that any contact with police will increase their risk of deportation. Others come from cultures that mistrust and fear law enforcement. People from Southeast Asia or the Middle East, where law enforcement often is used as a tool of oppression, are particularly less inclined to report hate crimes.[31]

In many cultures, being a victim of a bias-motivated crime carries a stigma. In fact, in some Asian communities, being a victim of a crime is thought to bring shame to a family. Some victims refuse to report a bias-motivated crime because they consider it a degrading personal experience, like a rape, and feel that filing a report will leave them exposed to further humiliation.[32]

Understanding Hate Crimes

Characteristics of Hate Crimes

Like other crimes, bias-motivated criminal acts have specific characteristics. The UCR for 1994 illustrates that the majority of hate crimes are committed by young white males against persons of other races, and the most common crimes involve simple assault or intimidation. Of the 7,144 bias-motivated offenses reported for that year, 5,115, or 72 percent, were crimes against persons, including 2,792 incidents of intimidation and 1,305 simple assaults. Thirteen persons were murdered in 1991 in bias-motivated attacks. Another 2,023 offenses were committed against property, with destruction, damage, or vandalism accounting for 1,734 incidents, or about 86 percent of the property incidents.

According to the UCR, approximately 60 percent of the hate crime incidents were motivated by racial bias; 18 percent by religious bias; 12 percent by a bias against sexual orientation; and 10 percent by a bias against ethnicity or national origin.

Most crimes against persons typically are committed by a family member or acquaintance. But when it comes to hate crimes, an attack is more likely to be committed by a stranger. In a study of 452 hate crimes reported to the Boston, Massachusetts, police, 85 percent involved offenders whose identity was not known to the victims; in contrast, one national study showed that about two-thirds of all violent crimes are committed by strangers.[33]

Among hate crime offenders, juveniles and young people are disproportionately represented. Nationally, slightly more than one-quarter of all crimes are committed by people younger than 20 years old, but about half of all hate crimes are estimated to be committed by people younger than 20.[34] According to a study funded by the Office of Juvenile Justice and Delinquency Prevention, an estimated 17 to 26 percent of all hate crime incidents recorded by law enforcement agencies are committed by juveniles.[35]

Perhaps the most salient characteristic of bias crimes is that they are more likely to involve a physical assault. While historically about 11 percent of all crimes are assaults against persons, for bias crimes assaults account for nearly one-third of total cases reported.[36]

Because they are more likely to involve assaults, hate crimes also are more likely to involve physical injuries. Offenders often use what hate crime experts call "imprecise weapons of opportunity," such as bricks, bats, clubs, tree limbs, and box cutters. As a result, hate crimes tend to be excessively brutal and result in more serious injuries than common criminal attacks.[37]

African Americans: Most Likely Victims

Historically, African Americans have endured the greatest brunt of hate crime incidents. Nearly 4 out of every 10 hate crime incidents in 1994 were classified as "anti-black." In more than half of all criminal incidents of racial bias that year, an African American was the victim. During the same year, 15 percent of all hate crimes were directed at Jews, and 11 percent were directed at gays.[38]

According to the UCR, the 2,988 anti-black hate crime incidents in 1995 represented a 4-year high. Part of the statistical increase in hate crimes against African Americans is a reflection of better reporting by both police and citizens. Yet better reporting does not account for all of the increase. Concluded one civil rights leader, "This Nation has not yet come to grips with race relations."[39]

As members of the largest minority group in the Nation, African Americans are mathematically more likely than members of other target groups to be victims of hate crimes. As of April 1995, there were 193.3 million non-Hispanic whites living in the Nation, accounting for 74 percent of the total U.S. population. African Americans numbered approximately 33 million, or 13 percent of the population, followed by Hispanics, with 26.8 million; Asian Americans or Pacific Islanders, 9.2 million; and American Indians/ EskimosAleutians, 2.2 million.[40]

African Americans also are burdened by a history of racial tension and violence that has its roots in the institution of slavery, the residual effects of which are being felt even today, 132 years after the Civil War. As a result of State and local laws and other sanctions that sprang up during and after Reconstruction, blacks continued to be discriminated against and segregated. Called "Jim Crow"—after a black character from a 19th-century song-and-dance act—this official and unofficial policy created a climate that encouraged organized racist groups to commit acts of terror and violence against blacks and reinforced false yet persistent stereotypes.

Despite the best efforts of governmental and private interests to foster a climate of tolerance and compassion in the Nation, racial stereotypes persist. A 1990 study by the National Opinion Research Center called "Ethnic Images" found that a majority of white respondents felt that blacks were lazier, less intelligent, more violent, and less patriotic than whites.[41]

While hate crimes traditionally had been directed at African Americans, hate violence committed by African Americans has been "escalating at an alarming rate," according to Klanwatch, a Project of the Southern Poverty Law Center. From 1991 to the end of 1993, 46 percent of all racially motivated homicides tracked by Klanwatch were committed by African Americans on white, Asian, or Hispanic victims. In 1990, by comparison, Klanwatch documented one racially motivated murder committed by an African American; the group documented no cases in 1989.[42]

Arsons at Black Churches

A rash of arsons at African-American churches in the South spurred the Federal Government to launch a major investigation that, by November 1996, had led to the arrest of 120 suspects. Of the 298 arson cases probed between January 1995 and November 1996, approximately 43 percent involved fires at black churches. Political and religious leaders say that, because white churches far outnumber black churches, the concentration of black church burnings indicates that the Nation is experiencing a serious wave of hate crimes.[43] One religious leader called the arsons "the greatest outbreak of violence against the black church since the height of the civil rights movement."[44]

Some 94 black churches burned in the South between January 1, 1995, and mid-November 1996, with Texas leading the Nation for the most attacks, followed by Tennessee, South Carolina, and Florida. Eighty-six Southern churches designated as "nonblack" were torched in the same period, although that figure could be lower: several houses of worship that were not designated as African American are Islamic mosques—whose members tend to be mostly black.[45]

Federal investigators are reluctant to estimate what portion of the total number of arsons at black churches appear to be racially motivated. Nearly two-thirds of the individuals arrested on charges of burning black churches are white, and about one-third are African Americans. Of the individuals arrested for setting arson fires at African-American churches, a few are card-carrying members of the Ku Klux Klan (KKK). But others include a 13-year-old girl who holds anti-Christian beliefs, a volunteer fireman who also is a pyromaniac, and many juvenile vandals. Overall, about 40 percent of the fires appear to have been started by juveniles.[46]

Investigators have found that racial hatred is only one of several motives behind the burnings. Some fires appear to be the work of "copycats," burglars covering their tracks, disgruntled church members, thrill-seekers, or the result of insurance scams. Many of the suspects apprehended thus far are economically disadvantaged, poorly educated, and abusers of alcohol.[47]

Federal officials first noticed a "spike" of black church arson reports in January 1996, around the birthday of slain civil rights leader Martin Luther King, Jr. The number of reports increased as news coverage intensified. Since the peak month of June, the number of reports has decreased slightly from six or seven a week to four or five a week.[48]

The spike occurred after a decade in which the overall number of church arsons appeared to be on the decline. According to the National Fire Protection Association (NFPA), a nonprofit organization that promotes fire safety, there were 1,420 church arson fires in 1980 compared with 520 in 1994—a decrease of 63 percent. Property damage caused by arson was estimated at $16 million in 1994, down from as high as $30 million in previous years. Since 1980, the annual number of reported church arsons increased in only two years—1984 and 1991. (Because of a five-quarter lag in the collection, reporting, and compilation of arson statistics, national church arson figures for 1995 are not expected to be ready until March 1997, according to the NFPA.)

Despite indications that the overall number of church arsons has been waning in the past decade, both civil rights leaders and hate crime experts say that public recognition of the church arson problem is long overdue. —[The church burnings] have brought out the race relations problem in this country," said one civil rights leader.[49]

Role of the Black Church

African-American churches have always been vulnerable to arson attacks. Many churches are small wood-frame structures located in isolated rural areas without smoke alarms, burglar alarms, or other security devices.[50]

The lack of amenities, however, masks the powerful role that churches historically have played in black communities. The influence of the black church was such that during the 18th and 19th centuries, many States and counties had laws that prohibited slaves from gathering for religious services because of fears that such gatherings might lead to spontaneous or organized insurrection.[51]

The first recorded arson destroying a black church occurred in South Carolina in 1822, and the practice persisted throughout the Civil War. Arson became a favorite tool of intimidation and destruction for racists during the civil rights movement of the 1950's and 1960's. Churches were popular targets because they often served as meeting places for activists seeking to end segregation or ensure voting rights.[52]

During those turbulent years, —Night Riders"—descendants of the night patrols that used to roam country roads enforcing curfews during slave times—terrorized the black community by firebombing black churches and homes. Night Riders were part of a well-organized effort to maintain segregation in the South that was largely orchestrated by members of the Knights of the Ku Klux Klan.[53]

Public Responses

The Center for Democratic Renewal, an organization that advocates the prosecution of racist groups such as the KKK, was one of the first organizations to bring the problem of church burnings to national attention. Shortly after the burning of three churches in the Boligee, Alabama, area in December 1995 and January 1996—and a spate of other fires in Louisiana and Tennessee—the organization, based in Atlanta, Georgia, began issuing regular reports on church burnings.[54]

Later, the New York-based National Council of Churches—whose director also sits on the board of directors of the Center for Democratic Renewal—also began issuing press releases about the church burnings. Soon, reporters from all of the major news organizations were converging on the town of Boligee and its 258 citizens, and each new arson report attracted national coverage. As church arsons grew in the Nation's consciousness, other civil rights and religious groups entered the fray.[55]

The Christian Coalition in April 1996 offered rewards of $25,000 to anyone who could provide information that would lead to the arrests of church arsonists. Less than 2 months later, Ralph Reed, director of the Christian Coalition, promised that his organization would raise at least $1 million to help rebuild black churches and would set up a special fund to provide alarms, motion detectors, outdoor flood lights, and smoke detectors for rebuilt churches. Reed also called for a day of national racial reconciliation, which was held on Sunday, July 14, 1996, at churches around the country.[56]

Meanwhile, the National Council of Churches launched a $4 million fundraising drive to rebuild black churches and assist multiracial congregations. By October, the organization, joined by the American Jewish Committee and National Conference of Catholic Bishops, had collected more than $6 million.[57] The National Black Evangelical Association and the National Association of Evangelicals—whose membership includes 52 Protestant denominations and thousands of independent churches—also established a rebuilding fund.[58] The 15.6-million-member Southern Baptist Convention, the Nation's largest Protestant denomination, reportedly raised $282,000 among delegates to its annual convention.[59]

When two former Klansmen were indicted on civil rights violations for allegedly conspiring to burn a South Carolina church in June 1995, the Southern Poverty Law Center filed a civil lawsuit on behalf of the church. The two had pleaded guilty to criminal charges for torching the Macedonia Baptist Church in Bloomville, South Carolina, and the Mount Zion AME Church in Greeleysville, South Carolina.

In its civil suit filed on behalf of Macedonia Baptist, the center alleges that the men were acting as agents of the KKK when they lighted the fires. Such a lawsuit represents the linchpin of a strategy that the organization has used successfully in similar cases of racial terror: holding a group financially responsible for the racist crimes of its members.[60]

Meanwhile, the U.S. Commission on Civil Rights held a series of public forums in seven Southern states to examine the conditions that contributed to the wave of arsons. The eight-member bipartisan panel published a series of reports summarizing the concerns and observations expressed at the forums. (A final report on the forums, part of a 5-year project that began in late 1991 to gauge the nature of race relations in the nation, is expected to be released in late 1997.)

The reports assert that the arsons reflect deep-seated racial animosity and segregation in the South but caution that racial hatred is just one of several explanations for the fires. ―We could not find a pattern as such or a conspiracy," said Melvin Jenkins, the commission's central States regional director. ―But we do know that some whites are involved and [that] the good ol' boy network is at work. And some of it boils down to a cluster effect— where you have several church arsons within a 100-mile radius."[61]

Federal Responses

To help church congregations rebuild in the aftermath of arsons and bring the perpetrators to justice, President Clinton launched a major Federal initiative in the summer of 1996. First, he ordered the Justice and Treasury departments to collaborate in a massive investigation of church arsons. More than 200 agents from Justice's Federal Bureau of Investigation and Treasury's Bureau of Alcohol, Tobacco and Firearms formed a task force, and hundreds more State and local law enforcement and fire officials formed regional task forces that operate out of U.S. attorneys' offices across the States.[62]

On July 3, Clinton signed the Church Arson Prevention Act of 1996 (H.R. 3525), which makes it easier to prosecute church arsons as Federal offenses.[63] The law enhances penalties for damaging religious property or obstructing any person's free exercise of religious freedom if the offense in some way affects interstate commerce. Previously, the provisions applied only when a suspect crossed State or national lines and the loss exceeded $10,000. The law also provides compensation to churches that fall prey to arsons and extends Federal hate crime and crime victim protections to churches attacked because of the ethnic or racial composition of their memberships.

In addition, the act directs the U.S. Department of Housing and Urban Development to guarantee private loans amounting to $5 million to rebuild destroyed churches and reauthorizes the Hate Crime Statistics Act of 1990, which directs the Justice Department to collect hate crime data from State and local jurisdictions.

On July 19, Clinton announced a national arson prevention initiative, instructing several Federal agencies to coordinate all available Federal, State, local, and private resources to foster arson prevention and establish an arson prevention clearinghouse.[64]

A week later, Clinton and leaders of eight national fire service organizations signed the President's Partnership for Fire and Arson Protection, which resulted in the publication of several church arson prevention brochures. Clinton also made $6 million available from the Justice Department through the Bureau of Justice Assistance to 1,291 communities in 13 targeted Southern States. The funds may be used to support efforts to enhance law enforcement, intensify surveillance of churches, hire additional employees, or reimburse overtime expenses.[65]

Other Targets of Hate Crimes

Two groups to experience a surge of hate crimes in the past 2 years are Asian Americans (including Pacific Islanders) and homosexuals. According to the UCR, the number of bias-motivated offenses targeting Asian Americans increased nearly 70 percent in 1995 compared with the previous year, from 209 incidents to 355 incidents, and 38 percent since 1993.[66] A civil rights group tracking hate crimes against Asian Americans reported 458 incidents in 1995, 452 incidents in 1994, and 335 incidents in 1993.[67]

Incidents against gays (including bisexuals) increased 51 percent in 1995 compared with the previous year, from 663 to 1,002 incidents. The number of incidents increased 20 percent since 1993, according to the UCR.[68]

Of all religious groups, Jewish people are most likely to be the targets of bias-motivated offenders. In 1995, offenses against Jews accounted for 1,058 of the 1,277 incidents involving a hatred for a particular religion, about 83 percent.[69] Because these crimes often involve vandalism against synagogues, schools, and cemeteries, Jews are more likely than other groups to report incidents to authorities.[70]

A Climate for Hate Crimes

A host of factors may create a climate in which people, motivated by their biases, take criminal action. Such factors include poor or uncertain economic conditions, racial stereotypes in films and on television, hate-filled discourse on talk shows or political advertisements, the use of racial code language such as ―welfare mothers" and ―inner city thugs," and an individual's personal experiences with members of particular minority groups. Once a climate of hate is created, a single incident can trigger a wave of hate crimes.

Consider the forces that led to the ―spike" in hate crimes during the early 1990's. The Nation was in the midst of an economic recession, and ―foreign" competition for jobs, sales markets, and resources increasingly were being cited as direct or indirect causes of the malaise. The year 1992 was also a presidential election year, and the electronic media was inundated with a continual stream of political messages, some of which seemed designed to stoke fear and resentment. Meanwhile, a surge of immigration was changing the racial makeup of the Nation, and many people were uncomfortable with the growing diversity.[71]

In addition, a public debate was raging over the appropriate role and cost of the Federal Government. In the print and electronic media, institutions of every kind were being ―bashed." Shock radio hosts were attracting a growing national audience and, in the process, changing the tone of civil discourse on social and political issues. One result was a growing acceptability of hateful discourse.[72] This combination of factors created a climate for hate crimes.

Trigger Incidents

Once a climate for hate crimes exists, all that is needed is a sensational, high-profile racial incident, called a —trigger incident," to set off a —cycle of retaliatory incidents or even civil disorder."[73] Two trigger incidents during the early 1990's were the videotaped beating of a black 25-year-old motorist and petty offender named Rodney King in March 1991, and the subsequent acquittal in April 1992 of four white Los Angeles, California, police officers accused in the assault. News of the acquittal sparked massive rioting, looting, vandalism, and fire setting in South Central Los Angeles. The following month, the level of hate crimes began to increase in many jurisdictions across the Nation.[74] Similarly, the highest level of bias-motivated incidents in New York City occurred during the month immediately following the attack on a group of black men in Howard Beach, New York.[75]

External Influences

Hate crime incidents are sensitive to external events. In the 1980's, when it seemed that Japan was cutting into American sales of automobiles and electronic equipment, there was an increase in attacks on Japanese.[76] During the Gulf War, there was an increase in attacks on Arab-Americans.[77] —There is a sense of retaliation. One thing happens and people want to get even. There is sort of a juvenile gang mentality. `They got one of ours; we'll get one of theirs,'" one researcher said.[78] After the Oklahoma City bombing, there was an initial outpouring of anti-Arab-American sentiment that threatened to escalate but was quelled when it became known that the chief suspects in the bombing were Caucasians born in the United States.[79]

Scapegoating

Some hate crime experts have noted that hate crimes tend to rise during times of economic uncertainty. In fact, a few say that a general correlation exists between the public's *perception* of the state of the economy and the level of hate crimes. —The *perception* of how things are is almost more important than the reality," one expert said.[80] Although some feel that the connection between hate crimes and the state of the economy is overstressed,[81] hate crimes do seem to increase during periods of economic uncertainty.[82] During these periods, minorities find themselves regarded as the cause of the negative conditions that others are experiencing. Such a climate gives rise to —scapegoating," the blaming of a minority group for the misfortunes of society as a whole.

Who Commits Hate Crimes?

Most hate crimes are committed not by members of an organized hate group but by individual citizens. A Louis Harris poll of 1,865 high school students conducted in 1990 found that more than half claimed that they had witnessed a racial confrontation —very often" or —once in a while." While few could be called members of organized hate groups, nearly half admitted that they had joined a bias-motivated confrontation or, at the very least, thought that the people being confronted were getting what they deserved.[83]

Some perpetrators resent the growing economic power of a particular racial or ethnic group and engage in scapegoating; others react to a perceived threat to the safety and property value of their neighborhood. The desegregation of public housing provides a good example of the latter. Research has shown that when the first nonwhite family moves into a white neighborhood there is a spike of bias-motivated incidents. The number of incidents wanes until minority saturation reaches about 20 percent, then it increases again. When minority saturation crosses 50 percent, there is a third spike of hate crimes incidents.[84]

Other offenders include the "thrill seekers"—those who randomly target interchangeable representatives of minority groups for harassment and violence—and the "mission offenders," those who believe they are on a mission to rid the world of some perceived evil. The last group, the "mission offenders," comprises less than 2 percent of bias-motivated offenders.[85] The majority of offenders—and passive observers—merely are individuals who believe racial and ethnic stereotypes and act upon spur-of-the-moment impulses. Frequently, alcohol or drug use is a factor.[86]

Significance of Hate Crime Statistics

While statistics may seem to indicate a low number of hate crimes compared with other types of crime, hate crime statistics carry more weight than statistics for other offenses. A bias-motivated threat or action not only victimizes the immediate target, it victimizes every member of the group that the immediate target represents.[87]

A single hate crime has the power to send a broad ripple of fear and discomfiture across a community. A "skinhead" who paints a swastika on the wall of a synagogue has not merely committed an act of vandalism; he has communicated a message of ethnic loathing to everyone within eyeshot, whether Jew or Gentile. He has scrawled a symbol that for many observers will invoke memories of concentration camps, Kristallnacht, the Holocaust, and World War II—a symbol that has galvanized and inspired dread among individuals and nations for more than 60 years.

Similarly, a racist who burns a cross on the front lawn of the home of an African-American family has not merely committed an act of arson and harassment; he has sent a racial message to everyone who hears of, reads about, or sees the event, whether they are black or white. He has committed an act that for many observers is bound to invoke memories of slavery, hangings, hooded Klansmen, school segregation, even the Civil War, and will undoubtedly stir up emotions ranging from fear of persecution to sadness over the persistent social divisions that plague the Nation.

Violent hate crimes are the most virus-like offenses in terms of the message they send and their psychological impact on members of the targeted group. Violent hate crimes often create tides of retaliation and counterretaliation that can spill into other minority groups and eventually may engulf an entire community. The month after the Howard Beach incident in 1986, when three African Americans were set upon by an angry young mob of whites, New York experienced possibly the highest –spike" of hate crime incidents in the city's history.[88] During and after the Los Angeles riots of 1992, sparked by the acquittal of four white police officers in the beating of Rodney King, vandals and looters destroyed or damaged dozens of businesses, including many Asian-American businesses.[89]

The simple truth about hate crimes is that each act victimizes not one person, but many. Each act connotes and denotes far more than the average criminal offense. It is in such a light that hate crime statistics must be viewed.

The Role of Hate Groups

Since the terrorist bombing of the Alfred P. Murrah Federal Building in
Oklahoma City, Oklahoma, in April 1995, the Nation has focused on a
growing antigovernment movement that seems to share some of the ideological precepts of certain organized hate groups, most notably white supremacists. Whether domestic terrorists are taking their inspiration or
orders from fringe militia groups or so-called —patriot" groups is open to
debate, but Federal law enforcement agencies and national groups that
regularly track hate crimes agree that the threat of domestic terrorism has
increased sharply in recent years. The FBI called 1995 —the year of the terrorist" and hired an additional 50 analysts to study both international and
domestic terrorism.[90]

More than 800 groups, including 441 self-styled militia units, have been
identified by the Southern Poverty Law Center as part of a growing —patriot movement." The Anti-Defamation League has estimated that militias,
with about 15,000 total members, are active in 40 States. Most of these
groups operate independently but are linked by a hatred of other groups
and government authorities. Among the groups that the center has linked
to the movement are white supremacists, Neo-Nazis, Klansmen, Freemen,
anti-abortion radicals, and Christian Identity (CI) followers.

Some experts assert that extremist groups are not necessarily growing in
size or number but in influence through their access to shortwave and
commercial radio frequencies, the vast and growing global cyberculture
of the Internet, and underground books, magazines, and music.[91]

A New Strategy

The historic image of a Ku Klux Klansman is of a robed and hooded figure
bearing a lighted torch. The word —skinhead" may evoke an image of a
shaved-head, tattooed young ruffian in black boots. Their appearances are
carefully designed to send unmistakable messages of alienation and threat.
Their rhetoric traditionally has been blatantly racist and defiant, and their
tactics of confrontation have become well known to law enforcement agencies. However, during the past decade, organized hate groups have been
evolving a new image that is more palatable to —middle America." At the
same time, they have been finding new ways of communicating to a larger,
more mainstream segment of society. Morris Dees, chairman of the Southern Poverty Law Center, notes the more recent tactics of Louis Beam, a
leader of the Aryan Nation and the KKK militia:

Beam and his militia followers are repackaging their message. They downplay racism and focus on people's fear and anger. The fear of, and anger at, a government that overregulates, overtaxes, and, at times, murders its citizens. . . . The fear of, and anger at, a government that takes away a person's right to bear arms so that the country is vulnerable to domination by a New World Order. Tens of thousands of people are hearing the message and thousands are joining the movement, many unaware that Beam and his fellow travelers are helping to set the agenda. . . . [Those joining] are mainly white and middle class. Most hold jobs, own homes, wear their hair short, don't use drugs, and, for one reason or another, they hate the government.[92]

Under the new strategy, racial violence rarely is ordered; rather it is tacitly sanctioned. The hate group exists to provide the ideological justification for violence. Instead of asking members to commit specific acts of violence—and risk the legal repercussions—these groups merely get out their message. Invariably, someone else, perhaps someone only tangentially connected to a hate group, will commit the offense.[93]

Experts also have observed a coalescing of traditional hate crime groups with fringe and extremist antigovernment groups, which may be supplying the ideological justification and inspiration for domestic terrorism.[94] Racist organizations such as the Aryan Nation already have in the past decade developed close ties to the militia movement and welded their message of white supremacy at all costs to the antigovernment, anti-gun-control sentiments expressed by most militia groups.[95]

The CI movement, described as a "ideology of racism, antisemitism, and male supremacy," has become the adoptive religion of the Freemen, a fringe group that in 1996 engaged in an 81-day standoff with FBI agents near Jordan, Montana, that ended peacefully with several arrests on charges of threatening to kidnap and murder a Federal judge, check fraud, and helping Federal fugitives avoid arrest. There is little doubt that some of the Freemen holed up in the 960-acre compound first heard CI's unorthodox Bible interpretations and the "truth about the white race" through satellite television programs, shortwave radio, the Internet, or videotapes and pamphlets.

The growing influence of the CI movement has prompted the Montana Association of Churches to start a program to educate citizens about the dangers of religious extremism. One researcher gave a talk to a women's Bible study group in Montana after several members ordered CI videotapes, thinking they would be receiving materials with a traditional Bible interpretation.[96]

Yet another piece of the new strategy is the concept of "leaderless resistance." Rather than organize themselves into the conventional pyramid structure favored by military forces and corporations, some hate groups

are reorganizing into secret or —phantom" cells of a few people, even
—one-man cells," that are difficult to detect and even more difficult to infil-
trate and control. Without a recognized leader or any central control or direction, the cells run less risk of exposure and can continue their activities
if other cells are exposed.[97]

A New Definition?

With the increasing influence of hate crime groups and the coalescence of
formerly disparate groups, the line between hate crimes and terrorism is
beginning to blur. In fact the rising influence of hate groups and the increase in acts of domestic terrorism have even led a few researchers and
political leaders to call for a new definition of hate crimes, one that might
include crimes motivated by a hatred of people, not because of their race,
national origin, sex, sexual preference, and religion but because of their af-
filiations or occupation.

While an assault on a lone homosexual person by a gang of teenagers on a
violent spree no doubt would be investigated, prosecuted, and reported as
a hate crime, there is little chance that an attack on an employee of the U.S.
Department of the Interior, Bureau of Land Management, by a group of
antigovernment —patriots" would be considered a bias-motivated crime
under any current definition.

Yet recent attacks on Federal workers, including the bombing of the Federal Building in Oklahoma City, are being viewed by some as hate crimes
committed against people who happen to work for the Federal Government. Testifying before the Senate Committee on the Judiciary, Emanuel
Cleaver II, mayor of Kansas City, Missouri, noted that his State had become —hotbed of militia activity." Urging Congress to expand the definition of hate crimes, Cleaver said, —When you look at what happened in
Oklahoma City, it clearly was a hate crime against workers of the Federal
Government."[98]

At a hate crime and terrorism planning meeting at the National Academy
of Sciences in Washington, D.C., a few dozen prominent researchers, aca-
demicians, and Federal experts in the fields of hate crimes and terrorism
struggled to identify the connections between hate crimes and terrorism.
They also sought to develop a definition of bias-motivated activity that
might embrace the concepts of both.

Jerome Skolnik of the University of California at Berkeley's School of Law
said that terrorism and hate crimes are similar in that they are both —deologically connected." Brent Smith, a criminal justice professor at the University of Alabama, however, pointed out that while both hate crimes and
terrorism include motive as an element of the offense, traditionally the motive in a terrorist act has been considered only during the sentencing phase
of a prosecution. William Chambliss, a sociologist who teaches at George

Washington University in Washington, D.C., suggested that such a definition might encompass any —deologically justified act."

Finally, the participants exhausted the issue of definitions. Other than to agree that hate crimes and terrorism share an —overlapping pathology and actors," they decided it was more important to concentrate their efforts on the best areas for research, such as identifying the differences between a hate group follower and someone who commits bias-motivated violence, and what actions might be taken to prompt a hate group follower to reject his racist, anti-Semitic, or antigovernment ideology. —We must try to understand what leads people in, what they do when they're in, and what leads people out," said Jerrold Post of George Washington University.

Hate Crimes and the Law

Jurisdictions across the Nation use three basic legislative approaches to combat hate crimes—prohibiting specific intimidating actions, prohibiting general behavior motivated by bias, and enhancing penalties for criminal acts motivated by bias.

A number of States, including California, Florida, and Ohio, have passed laws prohibiting specific activity at specific places, such as vandalism and intentional disturbances at places of worship. Florida and the District of Columbia have banned acts such as burning a cross or placing a swastika or other symbol on another's property with the intent to intimidate.

Other jurisdictions have passed legislation punishing any behavior that is motivated by bias. These statutes punish motive and criminal conduct as one offense. A New York hate crimes statute prohibits bias-motivated discrimination or harassment. —The targeted activity—the selection of a victim—is an integral part of the underlying crime," one State supreme court justice said in characterizing such statutes.[99]

Still other jurisdictions have passed statutes creating enhanced penalties when the motivation for an otherwise criminal act is bias. In Wisconsin, for example, State law provides that the maximum penalty for an offense is enhanced if the defendant intentionally selects the person against whom a crime is committed because of the —race, religion, color, disability, sexual orientation, national origin, or ancestry of that person."

Hate crime statutes may have significant elements in common with other State laws. For example, hate crime laws that include gender bias may overlap with domestic violence statutes—statutes that create specific penalties for criminal activity directed at family members and intimate partners. Multiple laws addressing similar conditions may create the opportunity to —tack" charges and improve the likelihood of a satisfactory conclusion to the case from the victim's viewpoint. However, overlapping statutes also may produce conflict concerning which charges should be brought in a highly political and sensitive case.

Hate crime statutes have been most frequently challenged on the grounds that they violate the first amendment of the U.S. Constitution, which restricts governments' power to make laws infringing upon an individual's freedom of speech and expression. Opponents of hate crime laws argue that punishing an offender more harshly when that person commits a crime because of a bias against a class of persons penalizes his or her thoughts and violates the first amendment. Such opponents consider hate crime laws to be —iewpoint discrimination" and challenge the grounds upon which the proponents of the laws rely as purely speculative. They assert, for example, that penalty enhancement cannot be justified on the grounds that injury to society is greater when a crime is motivated by bias. They claim that retaliatory crimes do not necessarily increase when crimes are bias motivated, citing examples of certain religious groups that, in accordance with the tenets of their religion, will not retaliate when attacked, and certain disabled persons who cannot retaliate. They also argue that all crimes, not only those motivated by bias, are dehumanizing and distressing to the victim; therefore, a rash of any type of crime, not just hate crime, is likely to generate community unrest and injure society as a whole.

Figure C: State Hate Crime Statutory Provisions[100]

	AL	AK	AZ	AR	CA	CO	CT	DC	DE	FL	GA	HI	ID	IL	IN	IA	KS	KY	LA	ME	MD	MA	MI	MN	MS	MO
Bias-Motivated Violence and Intimidation	I			I	I	I	I	I	I		I	I		I			I	I	I		I	I	I			
Civil Action			I	I	I	I	I		I		I	I		I			I				I			I		
Criminal Penalty	I			I	I	I	I	I	I		I	I		I			I	I	I		I	I	I			
Race, Religion, Ethnicity[101]	I			I	I	I	I	I	I		I	I	I	I			I		I		I	I	I			
Sexual Orientation				I			I	I		I			I		I			I				I				
Gender		I			I			I	I				I		I			I				I	I	I		
Other[102]		I		I			I	I	I			I	I	I				I				I				
Institutional Vandalism	I		I	I	I	I	I	I	I	I		I		I	I	I	I	I	I		I	I	I			
Data Collection			I		I		I	I		I			I	I		I			I	I		I				
Training for Law Enforcement[103]														I		I						I		I		

	MT	NE	NV	NH	NJ	NM	NY	NC	ND	OH	OK	OR	PA	RI	SC	SD	TN	TX	UT	VT	VA	WA	WV	WI	WY
Bias-Motivated Violence and Intimidation	I		I	I	I		I	I	I	I	I		I	I		I	I	I	I	I	I	I			
Civil Action					I		I			I	I	I	I	I			I	I		I		I			
Criminal Penalty	I		I	I	I		I	I	I	I	I		I	I		I	I	I	I	I	I				
Race, Religion, Ethnicity	I		I	I	I	I	I	I	I	I	I	I	I	I		I	I	I	I	I	I	I			
Sexual Orientation			I	I	I						I						I	I		I		I			
Gender				I	I		I		I									I		I	I	I			
Other					I		I				I						I		I		I	I			
Institutional Vandalism	I			I	I		I			I	I	I		I		I		I		I					
Data Collection					I	I				I	I	I	I			I			I						
Training for Law Enforcement										I	I											I			

Proponents of hate crime laws counter that hate crime statutes do not conflict with the tenets of the first amendment because they do not punish an individual for exercising freedom of expression but rather for motivation for engaging in criminal activity, a factor often considered when evaluating the seriousness of an offense. They maintain that when an offender has a biased motive, that offender's crime should carry a more severe penalty because the injury suffered by the victim and by society is greater. When the core of a person's identity is attacked, they contend, the degradation and dehumanization is especially severe, and additional emotional and physiological problems are likely to result.[104] Society in turn can suffer from the disempowerment of a group of people, say the proponents. Furthermore, they assert, the chances for retaliatory crimes are greater when a hate crime has been committed. The riots in Los Angeles, California, that followed the beating of Rodney King, a black motorist, by a group of white police officers are cited as support for this argument.

R.A.V. v. City of St. Paul, Minn.

The U.S. Supreme Court has addressed certain issues raised by first amendment scholars in two recent rulings on the constitutionality of hate crime legislation. In *R.A.V.* v. *City of St. Paul, Minn.*,[105] the Court in 1992 examined legislation that made particular bias an element of a crime.

R.A.V. was accused of burning a cross on a black family's lawn. He was charged subsequently under St. Paul's Bias-Motivated Crime Ordinance, which made it a misdemeanor to —place on public or private property a symbol, object, appellation, characterization, or graffiti, including, but not limited to, a burning cross or Nazi swastika, which one knows or has reasonable grounds to know arouses anger, alarm or resentment in others on the basis of race, color, creed, religion or gender."

The trial court dismissed the charges on the grounds that the ordinance violated the first amendment because it was impermissibly broad and regulated the content of the offender's speech. The Minnesota Supreme Court reversed the trial court's decision, holding that the ordinance prohibited —fighting words"—words that inflict injury or tend to incite immediate violence—which are not protected by the first amendment. The court further found that the regulation was tailored appropriately to serve the State's interest in protecting the community against bias-motivated threats to public safety and order.

In an opinion written by Justice Antonin B. Scalia, a majority of the U.S. Supreme Court reversed the Minnesota Supreme Court's ruling, finding that the ordinance unconstitutionally restricted speech on the basis of its content. Applying its free speech precedents to the St. Paul ordinance, the majority concluded that the ordinance applied only to —fighting words" that insult or provoke violence —on the basis of race, color, creed, religion, or gender." A jurisdiction may proscribe unprotected speech on the basis of its content, the Court held, but it may not select one area of speech to criminalize while leaving other areas unrestricted, unless the selection is content-neutral. Therefore, Scalia wrote, a jurisdiction may criminalize un-protected speech in a selective manner, as long as the selectivity is not ─conditioned upon the government's agreement with what the speaker may intend to say."

The Court noted that words that expressed hostility toward a person be-cause of his or her sexual orientation or political affiliation were not pro-hibited by the city ordinance. The Court wrote that because the ordinance restricted biases of a particular nature, it barred only those viewpoints that the city council found distasteful. Scalia asserted that the ordinance uncon-stitutionally allowed persons on one side of a debate to speak freely while restricting the other side's response. The majority held that a law prohibit-ing all fighting words communicated in a threatening manner, instead of proscribing all fighting words that convey messages of racial intolerance, would be constitutional. In this case, the Court ruled, the Minnesota ordi-nance went beyond permissible regulation and infringed upon the free speech rights of the defendant.

Wisconsin v. Mitchell

R.A.V. did not address the constitutionality of other types of hate crime legislation. In 1993, the Court provided clarification when it considered the constitutionality of a statute that enhanced the penalty for otherwise crimi-nal behavior motivated by prejudice.

In *Wisconsin* v. *Mitchell*,[106] a group of young African-American males, in-cluding Todd Mitchell, discussed a scene from the movie ─Mississippi Burning" in which white men beat a black boy who is praying. As the group left the apartment where they had gathered, Mitchell asked them if they were ─hyped up to move on some white people." A few minutes later a white boy approached the group from across the street. As the boy walked by, Mitchell prompted the others to attack him. He said, ─There goes a white boy; go get him." Mitchell counted to three and pointed to-ward the boy. The group ran toward the boy and beat him severely, ren-dering him comatose for 4 days.

Mitchell was convicted of aggravated battery, an offense that normally car-ried a penalty of 2 years' imprisonment. Because the jury found that Mitchell intentionally had selected his victim based upon the boy's race, however, the maximum sentence increased to 7 years. State law specifi-cally provides that a maximum penalty for an offense is enhanced if the defendant intentionally selects the person against whom the crime is com-mitted because of the ─racereligion, color, disability, sexual orientation, national origin, or ancestry of that person." Mitchell was sentenced to 4 years' imprisonment. He appealed his conviction and sentence, arguing that Wisconsin's penalty-enhancement provision violated the first amend-ment by punishing offensive thought.

On the day after the *R.A.V.* decision was issued by the U.S. Supreme Court, the Wisconsin Supreme Court issued a ruling in *Wisconsin* v. *Mitchell* that the State's hate crimes law violated the defendant's right to free speech. According to the court, the law violated the first amendment because the State imposed additional penalties solely because of the defendant's biased motivation in committing the crime. "A statute that is designed to punish personal prejudice impermissibly infringes upon an individual's first amendment rights," the court said. Relying on Scalia's majority opinion in *R.A.V.*, the court concluded that the hate crime law was unconstitutional because it singled out the defendant's biased thoughts and penalized him based upon the content of those thoughts.

The U.S. Supreme Court rejected this analysis and upheld the statute as constitutional. Chief Justice William Rehnquist, who wrote the *Mitchell* court's unanimous opinion, found that the St. Paul ordinance targeted expression, which is protected by the first amendment, while the Wisconsin statute is aimed at conduct not protected by the Constitution. Wisconsin's enhanced-penalty law created an increased penalty for illegal conduct inspired by the defendant's "bigoted motivations," according to the Court. While a particular bias was an *element* of the crime itself under the Minnesota ordinance, it was a *factor* to be considered during sentencing under the Wisconsin statute, said the Court.

Rehnquist said that, although a sentencing judge may not take into account the defendant's abstract beliefs, however obnoxious to most people, the Constitution does not preclude the admission of evidence concerning one's beliefs and associations at sentencing if those beliefs and associations are in some way related to the commission of the crime. Rehnquist explained that sentencing judges traditionally have considered a wide variety of factors in addition to evidence bearing on guilt, including a defendant's motive for committing the offense. For example, murder, if committed for financial gain, can be considered an aggravating factor under many States' capital sentencing statutes, said the Court. Moreover, the Court held, the first amendment permits admission of a defendant's statements to prove motive or intent, provided they are relevant and reliable.

The Court also held that the statute has no "chilling effect" on free speech. Rehnquist said that it would be highly unlikely that an individual would suppress his "bigoted" beliefs for fear that evidence of those beliefs would be used against him at trial if he committed a serious offense.

Other Decisions

Other State appellate and high courts considering the constitutionality of hate crime legislation since *Mitchell* have followed either *Mitchell* or *R.A.V.* without expressing difficulty in reconciling the two decisions.[107] These courts generally have upheld State statutes that punish specific behavior motivated by bias, and the U.S. Supreme Court has denied appeals of these decisions.[108] State courts have ruled that there is no meaningful difference between such statutes and the penalty-enhancement statute upheld in *Mitchell*. Both types of statutes punish a crime motivated by bias, the courts have held. Following this line of reasoning, the Maryland appellate court, for example, upheld a statute making it a crime to ―harass or commit a crime upon a person . . . because of that person's race, color, religious belief or national origin."[109] As the Supreme Court of Missouri summarized with regard to a similar statute, ―While [the statute] admittedly created a new motive-based crime, its practical effect is to provide additional punishment for conduct that is already illegal but is seen as especially harmful because it is motivated by group hatred. It is clear from *Mitchell* that enhanced punishment for criminal conduct on account of a defendant's motives of bias or hatred toward a protected group is consistent with the United States Constitution."[110]

Federal courts have upheld Federal hate crime legislation against first amendment challenges based on similar reasoning. In *United States* v. *Stewart*,[111] for example, the U.S. Court of Appeals for the Eleventh Circuit held that a defendant who burned a cross on a black family's front lawn was properly prosecuted under Federal civil rights laws including 42 U.S.C. 3631,[112] which prohibits intimidation motivated by the defendant's hatred for a characteristic of the victim such as race or gender. The court held that ―because such intimidation itself is unprotected conduct, under *Mitchell* the statute is not facially invalid." The court said the defendant's conduct in *Stewart* was different from a cross burning held to make a political statement. While in *Stewart* the defendant burned a cross to threaten and intimidate a black family, political statements are constitutionally protected expression, said the court.[113] The U.S. Supreme Court refused to hear an appeal in this case.

The most recent Supreme Court action on hate crimes occurred in February 1996, when the Court denied review of a Florida Supreme Court decision upholding the State's statute that prohibits burning a cross on another's property without the property owner or occupant's written permission.

In *T.B.D.* v. *Florida*[114], a delinquency petition was filed against T.B.D., a juvenile, charging him with placing a burning cross on private property without permission. Section 876.18 of the Florida Code provides that it is a misdemeanor for ―any person or persons to place or cause to be placed on the property of another in the State a burning or flaming cross, real or simulated, in whole or in part without first obtaining written permission of the owner or occupier of the premises to do so."

The trial court dismissed the petition on the grounds that the statute violated the first amendment. The appellate court affirmed and the State appealed to the Florida Supreme Court.

The State high court reversed the lower courts, ruling that the law impacts fighting words or threats, which are unprotected by the first amendment. Adopting some of its language from U.S. Supreme Court opinions, the court explained that —[t]hreats of violence can be regulated because government has a valid interest in _protecting individuals from fear of violence, from the disruption that fear engenders, and from the possibility that the threatened violence will occur'. . . [and] _[f]ighting words' . . . _by their very utterance inflict injury or tend to incite an immediate breach of the peace.'" The court commented that in light of the State's history of bru-tal violence connected to cross burning, —it is difficult to imagine a scenario more rife with potential for reflexive violence and peace-breaching."

The court said the Florida statute differed from the ordinance in *R.A.V.* in that it did not prohibit threats or fighting words on a particular subject matter. Furthermore, the statute is not overly broad because cross burning is —eminently proscribable under the first amendment," said the court.

One justice dissented arguing that the statute failed the *R.A.V.* standard because cross burning was not regulated in a neutral manner. In order to comply with *R.A.V.*, the legislature must ban all burnings and fires set on private property with the intent to intimidate or threaten, said the dissenting justice.

Although the first amendment debate continues in the prosecution of hate crimes, State and Federal legislative attempts to combat bias-motivated offenses generally have been successful.

The American Civil Liberties Union's Response

While some legal experts believe all hate crime laws jeopardize first amendment rights, the American Civil Liberties Union (ACLU), historically a defender of the civil liberties of individuals, has attempted to craft a distinction between legislation that unconstitutionally restricts freedom of speech and expression and that which punishes conduct that is *intended to harm or threaten*.

The ACLU opposed the St. Paul ordinance challenged in *R.A.V.* v. *City of St. Paul* but supports the U.S. Supreme Court decision upholding the statute in *Wisconsin* v. *Mitchell*. The national organization actually found itself opposing its own local affiliate when it filed an amicus, or friend of the court, brief in support of the Wisconsin law on behalf of the government.

The ACLU Board of Directors in January 1993 adopted a hate crime legislation policy. The ACLU historically has opposed legislation that would —punish the mere expression of thoughts, opinions or beliefs, including expressions . . . such as the advocacy of racial supremacy or religious bigotry." However, the organization believes that penalty enhancement laws,

—[i]f properly drawn . . . do not punish protected speech or associations; rather, they reflect the heightened seriousness with which society treats criminal acts that also constitute invidious discrimination and are intended to or have the effect of depriving persons of legal rights or of the opportunity to participate in their community's political or social life simply because of their race, religion, gender, national origin, sexual orientation, or other group characteristic."

Penalty enhancement laws are permissible for hate crimes, according to the ACLU, because these crimes —convey a constitutionally unprotected threat against the peaceable enjoyment of public places to members of the targeted group. That threat constitutes an additional ground for culpability on the part of the perpetrator and justifies additional legal sanctions."

Under the ACLU's standard, a statute passes constitutional muster if it focuses on conduct in which the perpetrator intentionally selects the victim on the basis of —invidiously discriminatory factors. When such statutes are vague, or overbroad, as in the case of *R.A.V.* v. *City of St. Paul*, the ACLU will oppose them." Hate crimes legislation —shold be limited to situations where the underlying criminal conduct involves harassment, injury, or threat of physical injury to the victim, or damage or threatened damage to the victim's property."

Daniel Katz, legislative counsel for the ACLU, cited Florida's hate crime statute, which has been upheld by the State supreme court, as an example of a —vey dangerous" law that clearly has been abused. Under the Florida law, expression can be the sole basis for offense enhancement. The Florida law elevates a crime to a hate crime when it —evidences prejudice." Said Katz: —You have suspects being charged under the hate crimes statute because they called a police officer a _cracker' while they were being arrested for some other crime."

Other Responses to Hate Crimes

Mounting economic pressures in the face of massive corporate layoffs and a growing multiculturalism as a result of unprecedented immigration—in recent years the annual number of legal and illegal immigrants has added 1.4 million people to the U.S. population[115]—have created a climate in which a single bias-motivated incident has the potential of triggering a major wave of violence and destruction. In this climate, policymakers at the State and Federal levels are seeking new strategies to foster understanding among races and other groups, measure terrorism and hate crime problems, prevent future incidents of terrorism and hate crime, bring the perpetrators of bias-motivated crimes to justice, and aid and support hate crime victims.

Government Responses

As of 1995, 39 States had enacted laws that address bias-motivated violence and intimidation, many of them based on a model statute developed by the ADL. Nineteen States had statutes mandating the collection of hate crime data.[116] Meanwhile, dozens of law enforcement agencies across the Nation had promulgated new policies and procedures that address hate crimes, using model policies drafted by, among others, the International Association of Chiefs of Police and the National Organization of Black Law Enforcement Executives.[117]

In the past 4 years, Congress and the Justice Department have approved several new initiatives designed to combat hate crimes and violence. Several initiatives became part of the 1992 reauthorization of the Juvenile Justice and Delinquency Prevention Act, as amended. Among the measures was a requirement that each State's juvenile delinquency prevention plan include a component designed to combat hate crimes, and another that OJJDP conduct a national assessment of youth who commit hate crimes.

In 1993, OJJDP allocated $100,000 for the study, which was designed to identify the characteristics of hate crimes and the victims and perpetrators of hate crimes. The Juvenile Hate Crime Study, conducted by researchers at West Virginia University, found that only six States, and seven major cities within those States, collect offense data that specify the age of hate crime offenders. The data from the six States revealed a wide variance in hate crimes that can be attributed to people under the age of 18—8.5 percent to 62.6 percent. From the data, researchers extrapolated that an estimated 17 to 26 percent of all hate crime incidents recorded by law enforcement can be attributed to juveniles.[118]

Other new initiatives to combat hate crimes and violence include:

0 The U.S. Department of Education, under its Safe and Drug-Free Schools and Communities Federal Activities Grants Program, in fiscal year 1996 made $2 million available to public agencies and private nonprofit organizations for developing and implementing innovative strategies designed to prevent and reduce the incidence of hate crimes in communities.

0 OJJDP provided a $50,000 grant for the development of a school-based curriculum to address prevention and treatment of hate crimes by juveniles. Education Development Center Inc. (EDC) developed a curriculum and pilot tested it in schools in Massachusetts, New York, and Florida. EDC in fiscal year 1996 worked to provide the curriculum and related training to school districts and juvenile justice agencies.[119]

0 The Justice Department's Office for Victims of Crime in 1993 funded a $150,000 training curriculum to improve hate crime responses by law enforcement and victim assistance professionals.

0 The Violence Against Women Act (VAWA), Title IV of the Violent Crime Control and Law Enforcement Assistance Act of 1994, allows victims of gender-based crimes to sue the perpetrator in either Federal or State court for money damages or injunctive relief.[120]

0 Another provision of the 1994 Crime Bill, the Hate Crime Sentencing Act (HCSA), requires the U.S. Sentencing Commission to increase penalties for perpetrators of hate crimes.[121]

0 Under a proposed research project, the FBI and Northeastern University's (Massachusetts) Center for Criminal Justice Policy Research would seek to develop strategies to increase HCSA data collection by State and local law enforcement officials.

The Justice Department's Community Relations Service (CRS), the only Federal agency that exists primarily to assist communities in addressing intergroup disputes, has played a unique role in helping to identify and prevent hate crimes. CRS participates in HCSA training sessions for hundreds of law enforcement officials from dozens of police agencies across the Nation[122] and assists schools and school districts in addressing racial tension and conflict through programs in peer mediation.[123]

In 1994, CRS staffers were dispatched to provide settlement services to 13,225 Cuban and Haitian entrants, and the agency continued to mediate in specific racially motivated conflicts across the Nation. In partnership with the Federal Law Enforcement Training Center (FLETC), CRS held regional classes on bias-motivated crimes at the New Jersey Police Academy and 50 other police departments. CRS expected to train another 125 police departments in fiscal year 1995.

CRS also developed the Prison Racial Tension Assessment Tool, which allows correctional administrators to gauge the amount of racial tension in a correctional facility and provides information on ways to reduce such tensions. The agency began testing the Intercultural Sensitizer instrument, a diagnostic and training tool, in collaboration with the Defense Equal Opportunity Management Institute. CRS's Central Regional Office coordinated conflict resolution and cultural diversity training for the National Organization of Black Law Enforcement Executives.

Under a cooperative agreement with CRS, the National Institute Against Prejudice and Violence has published two booklets, –Bias Incident Data Collection: A Guide for Communities and Organizations" and —Th Lawyer's Role in Combating Bias-Motivated Violence."

Organizational Responses

For the past decade, public interest organizations have worked independently and in tandem with government agencies to develop hate crime legislation, improve the enforcement of existing hate crime laws, prosecute and track hate crime offenses, and prevent the further spread of hate crimes.

The ADL has been involved in a number of youth intervention and hate crime education programs. In Massachusetts, for example, ADL staffers from the organization's Boston regional office and the A World of Difference Institute worked with the State attorney general's office to develop a Youth Diversion Project in which nonviolent offenders are diverted into alternative education and community service programs.[124]

Hate crime response experts—including representatives from the ADL— are helping to develop a model curriculum for use by FLETC for Federal, State, and local police officials. The ADL has been pressuring Congress to fund the training through FLETC's National Center for State and Local Law Enforcement Training.[125]

The NGLTF has provided staff support, literature, and technical assistance to community anti-violence projects and local gay and lesbian groups. Recently, for example, the organization provided literature and technical assistance to the Gay and Lesbian Anti-Violence Project in Washington, D.C. The NGLTF lobbies to have sexual orientation included in the lists of protected groups in State statutes and local ordinances. Beyond its routine support activities, the NGLTF intervenes in individual cases, keeps files on political candidates, and publishes a —scre card" that rates a candidate's support or opposition to gay and lesbian rights issues.

Increasingly, religious groups are recognizing the need to promote racial and cultural tolerance. One example is the Racial Reconciliation Initiative, sponsored by the National Black Evangelical Association and the National

Association of Evangelicals. Under the initiative, materials are disseminated that explain church-based multiculturalism and help Christians understand the source of conflicts among races.

A Closer Look at Responses in the States

A number of other initiatives have been undertaken in the States to respond to hate crimes. The following are descriptions of selected initiatives with contact information included.

Hate Crime Response Networks

In *Hate Crimes: The Rising Tide of Bigotry and Bloodshed*, Levin and McDevitt recommend the formation of coalitions united against bigotry. Just as there has been a coalescing of hate crime groups, so too must local governments, agencies, and organizations bind together to fight prejudice and bias-motivated violence. Whether they are called coalitions, networks, or associations, these groups serve as clearinghouses of information about rights and services, and focal points for resources. California, Massachusetts, and a few other States are setting up —hate crime response networks."

Selected Initiative:

California Association of Official Human Relations Agencies

The California Association of Official Human Relations Agencies, based in San Francisco, is in the process of developing regional hate violence response networks in 10 regions in California. The network is arranged like a wheel with many spokes. At the hub is a human rights commission or other appropriate public agency or nonprofit organization that acts as a fiscal agent and/or designates staff to coordinate the project. A series of committees constitute the —spokes of the network structure, each representing and named after a different focus area, such as community activities, criminal justice, schools, the media, and youth. A community committee's members might include religious institutions, conflict resolution providers, civil rights organizations, neighborhood associations, or private sector representatives. A criminal justice committee's membership might include representatives of the police, district attorney, city attorney, attorney general, civil rights organizations, attorneys, and victims support groups.

Contact Information:

California Association of Human Relations Organizations
965 Mission Street, Suite 540
San Francisco, CA 94103
(415) 543–9741

Tracking Hate Crimes

As part of a study conducted in 1992, Brian Levin—then of Stanford University's (California) law school and the Center for the Study of Ethnic and Racial Violence in Edgewater, Colorado—placed jurisdictions that collect hate crime statistics into two broad groups. The first group is the core group of jurisdictions that have the most reliable data collection systems. These are the jurisdictions that have kept data for at least 3 years and have at least 100 incidents per year (Los Angeles County, California; San Francisco, California; Connecticut; Florida; Chicago, Illinois; Maryland; Boston, Massachusetts; Minnesota; New Jersey; New York, New York; Oklahoma; Oregon; and Pennsylvania).

In the second tier are jurisdictions that have smaller sample sizes, that have made changes in collection methods, that have unusual calendar cutoffs, or that have been collecting data for less than 3 years (Colorado; Delaware; District of Columbia; Idaho; Maine; Massachusetts, excluding Boston; Michigan; Montana; Rhode Island; Texas; Virginia; Washington; Wisconsin; and Wyoming).[126]

Recently, several States have taken steps to improve their hate crime reporting efforts. In North Carolina, for example, the State Department of Justice has created a new hate crime data collection strategy. Under the new program, the Division of Criminal Information (DCI) invites law enforcement agencies to sign a memorandum of understanding that the agency will report HCSA data in return for training by the North Carolina Justice Academy and DCI technical assistance.

Selected Initiatives:

New Jersey Uniform Crime Reporting Unit
New Jersey Office of Bias Crime and Community Relations

Considered a model State for bias crime reporting and enforcement, New Jersey takes a two-pronged approach to identifying bias-motivated crimes and enforcing bias crime statutes. The New Jersey Uniform Crime Reporting Unit of the State police has, since 1988, collected county-by-county data on hate crime statistics from all police agencies in the State and published an annual bias incident report. Agency reporting is mandated by State law. The State's Office of Bias Crime and Community Relations, part of the New Jersey Department of Law and Public Safety, Division of Criminal Justice, assists law enforcement agencies in the investigation and prosecution of bias-motivated incidents; facilitates educational and training programs that aid law enforcement agencies in the investigation and prevention of hate crimes; and facilitates community relations, conflict resolution, and cultural diversity.

Contact Information:

New Jersey Department of Law and Public Safety
Division of Criminal Justice
Office of Bias Crime and Community Relations
25 Market Street—CN 085
Trenton, NJ 08625–0085
(609) 984–1936

New Jersey Department of Law and Public Safety
Division of State Police
Uniform Crime Reporting Unit
Post Office Box 7068
West Trenton, NJ 08628–0068
609) 882–6920

Responding to Reported Incidents[127]

Rapid and effective responses to hate crimes show the community that law enforcement will take reports of potential hate crimes seriously. The extra attention given to the problem encourages other victims to report the crimes.

Because victims are hesitant to report hate crimes either out of embarrassment or fear, many agencies have established an integrated hate crime response network to aid them in receiving reports and responding effectively. Networks often include liaisons to local prosecutors, human rights commissions, and community-based victim advocacy organizations. Through the network, concerned community members may work with the police by supporting the victims and encouraging them to report crimes.

Community-based groups and victim support organizations work with law enforcement agencies in urging citizens to report hate crimes to help reduce the victim's sense of vulnerability and isolation.

Selected Initiatives:

Montgomery County (Maryland) Human Relations Commission

The Montgomery County Human Relations Commission (HRC) is a 15-member board charged with researching, assembling, analyzing, and disseminating pertinent data and educational materials that support activities and programs designed to help eliminate prejudice, intolerance, bigotry, and discrimination. HRC also institutes and conducts educational and other programs, meetings, and conferences to promote equal rights and initiates, receives, investigates, and seeks conciliation of discrimination complaints from residents. Among the programs operated by HRC are the Network of Neighbors and Network of Teens, which recruit and train citizens to provide peer support to victims of hate or violence in their communities and schools. Staff members provide support, refer victims to support and counseling services, provide translation services, and accompany victims to court. HRC also conducts a program to educate juveniles who have committed acts of hate or violence.

Contact Information:

Montgomery County Government
Human Relations Commission
164 Rollins Avenue
Rockville, MD 20852
Administration: (301) 468–4260
Complaints: (301) 468–4265

Anti-Defamation League

The Anti-Defamation League publishes a book listing cities that have departments and programs specifically dealing with bias crimes.

Contact information:

Anti-Defamation League
823 United Nations Plaza
New York, NY 10017
(212) 490–2525

Court Monitoring

Volunteers in some communities watch their local court system carefully for biased decisionmaking. Court monitoring groups analyze court performance and meet regularly with court leaders to make suggestions. The watch groups publicize their findings through the press and public hearings.

For the program to work, volunteers must be impartial and comment on the performance of the court, not on the outcomes of particular cases. The Women's Bar Association of Maryland started a court monitoring program after a report by the Joint Committee on Gender Bias in the Courts showed gender bias to be a problem in the Maryland court system. The National Center for State Courts supports self-monitoring of court systems and has published a manual that describes how a court can establish self-monitoring commissions.

Contact information:

Court Watchers
The Women's Bar Association of Maryland
520 West Fayette Street
Baltimore, MD 21201
(410) 528–9681

National Center for State Courts
300 Newport Avenue
Williamsburg, VA 23187
(757) 253–2000

Diversity and Tolerance Education

Tolerance education in elementary schools is being used across the country to help children relate to others from different backgrounds and cultures. Sociologists have said that children recognize racial and sexual differences early in life, and that by age 12 they have already developed stereotypes. Effective programs, therefore, target children ages 4 to 9.

Classroom exercises vary from newsletters written for a certain age group to theatrical productions and role playing. However, lessons students learn in the classroom need to be reinforced through parental involvement.

The Green Circle Program based in Philadelphia, Pennsylvania, strives to promote awareness, understanding, and appreciation of diversity in groups and schools across the United States. In 1992, the American Bar Association's Young Lawyers Division (YLD) launched four tolerance education pilot programs in elementary schools, middle schools, high schools, and colleges throughout the country. The programs featured education about the law, open discussions, and mock trials to give students a greater understanding of prejudice and discrimination.

The South Carolina Bar YLD sends attorneys to teach children in third and fourth grades. Students participate in mock trials and open discussions.

Contact Information:

American Bar Association, Young Lawyers Division
750 North Lake Shore Drive
Chicago, IL 60611
(312) 988–5000

South Carolina Bar, Young Lawyers Division
205 North Irby Street
P.O. Box 107
Florence, SC 29503
(803) 662–6301

Green Circle Program
1300 Spruce Street
Philadelphia, PA 19107
(215) 893–8400

Selected Initiative:

New Jersey Prejudice Reduction Education Program

To help young people deal with social problems and to teach racial tolerance, the New Jersey Departments of Law and Public Safety and Education have developed a special school curriculum called the Prejudice Reduction Education Program (PREP). PREP teaches prejudice reduction and conflict resolution and is designed to be used in the secondary schools. The curriculum is organized into four areas: Law and Values, the Nature of Prejudice, the Effects of Prejudice, and Developing Individual Coping Skills. The program curriculum explains the nature and sources of prejudice; provides examples of antisocial behavior and the destructive philosophy of hate groups; explains the nature and motivations of stereotyping, discrimination, and scapegoating; provides examples of prejudice that have resulted in discrimination; teaches critical social skills such as empathy and resisting negative peer pressure; and teaches techniques for resolving conflicts.

Contact Information:

Mr. Chuck Davis
Public Information Officer
The New Jersey Department of Law and Public Safety
Justice Complex
Trenton, NJ 09625
(609) 292–4791

Multilingual Reporting and Education Services

Employing bilingual police officers and posting bilingual notices will help bridge both language and cultural gaps between law enforcement agencies and immigrants who do not speak English. By reaching out to the immigrant communities, law enforcement can better protect minority groups that might otherwise fear police and make them more comfortable about reporting crime.

Some States provide funding for law enforcement agencies to hire bilingual officers or provide education on preconceptions that immigrants may have about law enforcement. Substations, police stations located in the immigrant community with community service officers (CSO's), give residents easier access to officers.

Selected Initiative:

Garden Grove (California) Police Community Service Officers

The Garden Grove Police Department in California received a grant from the State to hire two bilingual CSO's and to create substations in the midst of ―Little Saigon," where about 70,000 Vietnamese immigrants live. In addition to being present in the community and schools to speak about crime prevention, the CSO's also host a question-and-answer radio program in Vietnamese, which has received an overwhelmingly positive response.

Contact Information:

Community Service Officer
Garden Grove Police Department
P.O. Box 3070
11301 Acacia Parkway
Garden Grove, CA 92642
(714) 539–2284

Youth Leadership and Empowerment Programs

Several trial programs across the Nation are offering youth educational and skill development programs with advising sessions. The programs are culturally based to match the needs and customs of the community. However, program directors must work hard to gain the community members' support and confidence since residents are often skeptical of outside officials who enter the community.

The Martin Luther King Community Services in Freeport, Illinois, targets mostly African-American children living at or below the poverty line. The goal of the program is to reduce risks in the children's lives through educational programs, parent training and support, and partnerships in the community. The program provides after-school supervision and academic assistance.

Contact Information:

Martin Luther King Community Services of Illinois
Freeport Initiative
511 South Liberty
Freeport, IL 61032
(815) 233–9915

Police-Minority Partnerships and Associations

Ethnically oriented community organizations help create partnerships with law enforcement agencies to bridge the cultural and language barriers that exist between ethnic groups. These organizations help immigrants understand the history and customs of the United States, in addition to educating the rest of the community on immigrants' traditions and lifestyles. A liaison from each ethnic group in the community is responsible for such tasks as translating documents and human service information, providing mediation services, and coordinating events such as multicultural festivals for the whole community.

Selected Initiatives:

Lincoln Police Department's Vietnamese Outreach

Law enforcement agencies in Lincoln, Nebraska, have reached out to the Vietnamese community through various community events aimed at cultural awareness. For example, they held a school festival in which students had the opportunity to experience foods, dances, and costumes of other cultures. Since implementing the cultural awareness program in the community, Lincoln has recorded a decrease in racially motivated crimes.

Contact Information:

Community Liaison
Lincoln Police Department
233 South 10th Street
Lincoln, NE 68508
(402) 441–6350

Pennsylvania Alliance for Community and Law Enforcement Relations

To identify strategies to reduce tensions between minorities and law enforcement agencies, Pennsylvania Governor Tom Ridge (R) in March 1996 ordered the formation of a 20-member commission composed of minority leaders, community activists, religious leaders, law enforcement officers, and State and local government officials. Called the Alliance for Community and Law Enforcement Relations, the commission will be chaired by State Attorney General Thomas W. Corbett. The Alliance will gauge the effectiveness of State social programs, identify community strategies that already are working well, and target areas that need strengthening. Members will develop recommendations for policy development, resource allocation, and coordination of public and private efforts. Between 1988 and 1993, hate crimes in Pennsylvania reportedly increased by 130 percent. Forty-six percent of the victims were African American, while African Americans make up 9 percent of the State population.

Contact Information:

The Honorable Thomas Corbett
Attorney General
State of Pennsylvania
Strawberry Square, 16th Floor
Harrisburg, PA 17120
(717) 787–3391

Diversity Awareness Media Campaigns

The news media can help educate the public about other cultures, thereby decreasing prejudice. Community and religious leaders work together to persuade local newspapers and television stations to cover cultural festivals and produce specials and documentaries to acquaint residents with the customs and cultures of their neighbors.

Selected Initiative:

Anti-Defamation League's A World of Difference Program

The ADL's Boston office in 1985 started the —AWorld of Difference" program, which links media and educational resources to develop diversity awareness programming used in elementary and secondary schools, colleges, workplaces, law enforcement agencies, and community organizations. The ADL in Washington, D.C., together with WUSA–TV, created a program focusing on multicultural education training for teachers through live specials, documentaries, and other programs. The ADL has been invited to establish —AWorld of Difference" programs in Germany, Russia, and South Africa.

Contact Information:

Anti-Defamation League
1100 Connecticut Avenue NW., Suite 1020
Washington, DC 20036
(202) 452–8320

Community-Based Dispute Mediation Services

Conflict management programs provide mediation services to prevent disputes from escalating into larger community problems. Community-based mediators are recruited and trained in conciliation measures that attempt to resolve arguments peacefully. Disputing parties come to the program voluntarily or are referred from another organization. The small claims court, the police, the juvenile probation department, other city agencies, and schools refer individuals to the program.

Selected Initiative:

San Francisco Community Board Program

The Community Board Program in San Francisco, California, has grown from 20 volunteer mediators in 1977 to 300 volunteers currently and has provided mediation services to approximately 25,000 people. The program also has created conflict resolution training programs for schools, local government agencies, juvenile corrections facilities, and public housing committees.

Contact Information:

Community Board Program
Conflict Resolution Resources
1540 Market Street, Suite 490
San Francisco, CA 94102
(415) 552–1250

Support for Victims

Programs to help the victims of hate crimes are just as important as educational programs for offenders. Support services must be made available to help victims cope with the emotional, physical, and financial impacts of bias-motivated crimes.

Selected Initiative:

Horizons Anti-Violence Project

The Horizons Anti-Violence Project has been serving Chicago's gay, lesbian, and bisexual community since 1988. The group runs a 24-hour crisis line and refers victims to attorneys, counselors, and therapists. The project also provides court advocates for victims who press charges.

To prevent future crimes from occurring, the Horizons project sponsors community forums instructing residents how to protect themselves from violence and avoid conflicts. Horizons also provides training sessions through the police department on how to respond to hate crime incidents and works with the State's attorney's office to draft hate crime laws.

Contact Information:

Horizons Anti-Violence Project
961 West Montana
Chicago, IL 60614
(312) 472–6469

Counseling Offenders

A counseling program for young members of hate crime groups helps dispel attitudes that lead to criminal behavior through education about those ethnic groups that are the object of their hate. The purpose of the program is to broaden the offenders' views of other cultures and in doing so, to change their values. The counseling includes an encounter session at which hate crime offenders come face-to-face with members of minority groups. Offenders also visit county prisons and juvenile facilities to which they could be sentenced if they commit a hate crime.

Selected Initiative:

The Juvenile Diversion Project

The Juvenile Diversion Project, operated by the ADL, is a sentencing option for underage offenders in New York City family courts. Through a 20-hour educational program, students hear guest speakers from other cultures, visit synagogues and churches of other religions, and hear stories from bias victims. The curriculum, which involves take-home assignments and weekly readings, varies with the nature of the offense. After the classroom sessions are completed, an offender must complete 10 to 15 hours of community service in the community that was the target of his or her actions.

The program was based on a similar ADL Boston project that boasts that its graduates have had no further arrests for hate crimes; the Juvenile Diversions Project shows similar results. Program graduates from the first group of offenders have had no further arrests for any type of crime. Furthermore, the graduates have become leaders in the fight against bias, according to Associate Director Eliot Hoff.

Contact Information:

Eliot B. Hoff
Associate Director
New York Regional Office, Anti-Defamation League
823 United Nations Plaza
New York, NY 10017–3560
(212) 885–7974

Other Suggestions

"Trickle-Up" Effect

To most advocacy organizations, the failure to report a hate crime is nearly as bad as the offense itself. —Underreporting masks the true extent of hate crime activities, which encourages the perpetrators to continue their bigoted behavior and encourages similar behavior among their friends and associates," said Leiberman.[128]

When law enforcement officers are trained to identify, respond to, and report hate crime incidents, the result is that more hate crimes actually are reported, responded to, and prosecuted. The investigation and prosecution especially of notorious or high-profile hate crimes causes a trickle-up effect that tends to promote even more reporting by victims and witnesses.[129]

According to the ADL, the trickle-up effect begins with the officer who responds to a hate crimes report. The officer sets the proper tone for a thorough investigation and prosecution if he or she is able to —identify a hate crime, respond to it appropriately, and report it accurately." If police verify a hate crime and conduct followup inquiries, —prosecutors . . . should be expected to press hard for convictions" and —judges should then be under scrutiny to provide substantial sentences after convictions." If potential victims know a reporting system is in place and see a well-publicized case result in a stiff sentence for the perpetrators, they will be more likely to report a hate crime in the future.[130]

Thus, collecting and acting upon bias-motivated incident data serves a number of purposes such as making victims feel that someone is aware of their problem; creating opportunities for referrals to victim assistance services; encouraging reporting by individuals who might not otherwise notify police; providing police with information on potential trouble spots of hate group activity to allow for early intervention; and increasing public awareness of the issue.

Because reporting under the HCSA is voluntary, "the credibility of the national numbers is determined by the level of participation by State and local law enforcement agencies."[131] Law enforcement agencies representing more than 40 percent of the American population did not participate in the HCSA in 1994, and the vast majority of agencies that did participate reported zero hate crimes for that year. Of the 7,298 participating departments, only 1,150 reported even one hate crime.

The increased number of participating agencies indicates that "the FBI has done a good job in its initial outreach and education on the need to identify, report, and respond to hate violence," Strassler and Foxman said in their joint statement. "This year's figures, however, are incomplete—especially from such significant States as California, Massachusetts, and Illinois." The low numbers "indicate a need to reaffirm our national commitment to hate crime data collection efforts—and to aggressive enforcement of hate crime laws."

The ADL has urged that the HCSA be made permanent to ensure that hate crime data collection remains a part of the UCR. The ADL also wants the administration and Congress to take measures to ensure that the FBI continues hate crime training and education outreach efforts among field agents and that the FBI receives sufficient funding to continue to educate and train State and local law enforcement agencies about hate crimes.

To encourage HCSA participation at the State and local levels, the ADL urges Congress to provide incentives to State and local governments and law enforcement agencies, including national recognition, matching grants for training, a network to promote replication of successful programs, and awards for exemplary departments.

The organization also favors making participation in the HCSA program a prerequisite for receiving funds through the Justice Department's Office of Community Oriented Policing Services (COPS) or technical assistance grants from the Justice Department's Office of Justice Programs. "Hate violence can be addressed effectively through a combination of presence, prevention, and outreach to the community that is the hallmark of community policing," Arent said. "Congress and the administration should insist that new officers hired and trained under the COPS initiative begin to receive training in how to identify, report, and respond to hate violence.

"The long-term impact of the HCSA will be determined at the local level; and it will be measured not just by the aggregate numbers compiled by the FBI each year, but also by the improved response of law enforcement officials to each and every criminal act motivated by prejudice in communities across America. These numbers do not speak for themselves—because behind each of these figures are real people who have suffered physical and emotional trauma."[132]

In the fight against prejudice and hate crimes, the criminal justice system can have only a limited impact. Levin and McDevitt noted that —he criminal justice system—even when it operates at maximum effectiveness—is limited in its ability to stem the rising tide of bigotry and bloodshed. Solutions that work will require that our leaders lay the groundwork by long-term planning to reduce both intolerance and resentment."[133]

The authors believe that measures must be taken to reduce the sources of resentment among groups that feel they are being deprived of the benefits they believe other groups are attaining through affirmative action. For example, some low-income whites might feel less disenfranchised by affirmative action programs and policies if they were based on residence instead of race. Colleges and universities, for example, could change their image —from that of exclusivity to access" if they provided scholarship programs that —address the needs of lower-income families in the neighborhoods in which the particular [schools] are located."[134]

Notes

1. Mark S. Hamm, —Ŧrrorism, Hate Crimes, and Anti-Government Violence: A Preliminary Review of the Research" (background paper for National Research Council, Commission on Behavioral and Social Sciences and Education, Committee on Law and Justice, March 1996), pp. 1–2.

2. Jack Levin and Jack McDevitt, *Hate Crimes: The Rising Tide of Bigotry and Bloodshed* (New York: Plenum Press, 1993), pp. 1–8, 75, 86–87.

3. Hamm, p. 11.

4. Hamm, p. 12.

5. Hamm, p. 10.

6. Testimony of Charles W. Archer, Assistant Director, Criminal Justice Information Services Division, Federal Bureau of Investigation, U.S. Department of Justice, before the Senate Committee on the Judiciary (March 19, 1996).

7. Archer testimony.

8. Archer testimony.

9. Stephen Labaton, —Poor Cooperation Deflates FBI Report on Hate Crimes," *New York Times*, January 6, 1993, p. A10.

10. Colorado, Idaho, Iowa, Massachusetts, Michigan, North Dakota, South Carolina, Utah, Vermont, and Virginia.

11. The U.S. Department of Commerce, U.S. Department of Defense, and the FBI.

12. Telephone interview with Jack McDevitt, co-director, Center for Criminal Justice Policy Research, College of Criminal Justice, Northeastern University (April 18, 1996).

13. Levin and McDevitt.

14. Federal Bureau of Investigation, *Hate Crime Statistics, 1992* (Washington, D.C.: U.S. Department of Justice, 1993); *Hate Crime Statistics, 1993* (Washington, D.C.: U.S. Department of Justice, 1994); *Hate Crime Statistics, 1994* (Washington, D.C.: U.S. Department of Justice, 1995); *Hate Crime Statistics, 1995* (Washington, D.C.: U.S. Department of Justice, 1996).

15. McDevitt interview; Telephone interview with Brian Levin, Counsel, Klanwatch, a project of the Southern Poverty Law Center (March 14, 1996); Anthony Fainberg, "Terrorism and Hate Crimes in the U.S.: Prospects for the Nineties and Government Responses" (background paper for National Research Council, Commission on Behavioral and Social Sciences and Education, Committee on Law and Justice, March 1996), p. 6.

16. NGLTF Policy Institute, *Anti-Gay and Lesbian Violence, Victimization, and Defamation Report for 1991* (Washington, D.C., 1991).

17. NGLTF Policy Institute, *Anti-Gay and Lesbian Violence in 1994: National Trends, Analysis, and Incident Summaries* (Washington, D.C., 1995).

18. National Asian Pacific American Legal Consortium, *Audit of Violence Against Asian Pacific Americans* (Washington, D.C., 1994).

19. Interview with Michael Lieberman, Associate Director/Counsel, ADL's Washington, D.C., office (February 20, 1996).

20. Telephone interview with Helen Gonzales, Public Policy Director, NGLTF (March 7, 1996).

21. McDevitt, p. 12; NGLTF Policy Institute, *Anti-Gay and Lesbian Violence, Victimization, and Defamation Report for 1994* (Washington, D.C., 1994), p. 12.

22. Archer testimony.

23. Testimony of Bobby Moody, Chief of Police in Covington, Georgia, and Second Vice President of the International Association of Chiefs of Police, before the Senate Committee on the Judiciary (March 19, 1996).

24. Michael Lieberman, "Federal Action to Confront Hate Crimes: Preventing Violence and Improving Police Response," *New Challenges: The Civil Rights Record of the Clinton Administration Mid-term* (Washington, D.C.: Citizens' Commission on Civil Rights, 1995), pp. 217-229.

25. Testimony of Stephen Arent, Vice Chairman, ADL, National Civil Rights Committee, before the Senate Committee of the Judiciary (March 19, 1996).

26. Levin and McDevitt, p. 201.

27. Gonzales interview.

28. Gonzales interview.

29. Gonzales interview.

30. Gonzales interview.

31. Brian Levin, "Bias Crimes: A Theoretical and Practical Overview," *Stanford Law and Policy Review* (Winter 1993–94); Levin interview.

32. Levin interview.

33. McDevitt interview.

34. Levin interview.

35. Eric Bishop and Jeff Slowikowski, ―Hate Crime," *Fact Sheet #29* (Washington, D.C.: U.S. Department of Justice, Office of Juvenile Justice and Delinquency Prevention, August 1995).

36. Levin, ―Bias Crimes."

37. Levin interview; Levin, ―Bias Crimes"; *Office for Victims of Crime, National Bias Crimes Training for Law Enforcement and Victim Assistance Professionals: A Guide for Training Instructors* (Washington, D.C.: U.S. Department of Justice, 1995), p. 61.

38. Federal Bureau of Investigation, *Hate Crime Statistics, 1994.*

39. Telephone interview with Melvin Jenkins, Central States Regional Director, U.S. Commission on Civil Rights (November 14, 1996).

40. *The World Almanac and Book of Facts* (New York, 1996), pp. 382–386.

41. Klanwatch, a Project of the Southern Poverty Law Center, ―The Dynamics of Youth, Hate and Violence," *Klanwatch Intelligence Report* (Montgomery, Alabama, October 1995), p. 12.

42. Robert Kapler, ―Number of Hate Crimes by Blacks Rising, Rights Group Says," *Justice Research* (Washington, D.C.: National Criminal Justice Association, November/December 1993), p. 3.

43. Jenkins interview.

44. Eric Harrison, ―Christian Coalition Offers Blacks Repentance, Funds," *Los Angeles Times*, June 19, 1996, p. A1, quoting Ralph Reed, director of the Christian Coalition.

45. Telephone interview with Richard Jerome, Special Assistant to the Assistant Attorney General, U.S. Department of Justice, Civil Rights Division (November 15, 1996).

46. Jerome interview.

47. Jerome interview.

48. Jerome interview.

49. Jenkins interview.

50. Interview with Charles R. River, Press Officer, U.S. Commission on Civil Rights (November 13, 1996); Eric Harrison, ―Black Churches Have Long Been Targets," *Los Angeles Times*, June 15, 1996, p. A1.

51. Harrison, *Los Angeles Times*, June 15, 1996, quoting C. Eric Lincoln, Professor Emeritus of Religion at Duke University.

52. Harrison, *Los Angeles Times*, June 15, 1996.

53. Harrison, *Los Angeles Times*, June 15, 1996; Klanwatch, a Project of the Southern Poverty Law Center, *The Ku Klux Klan: A History of Racism and Violence* (Montgomery, Alabama, 1991).

54. David Crumm, "Truth Emerges From a False Crisis," *Detroit Free Press*, September 3, 1996, p. A7.

55. Crumm, *Detroit Free Press*, September 3, 1996.

56. Harrison, *Los Angeles Times*, June 19, 1996.

57. Harrison, *Los Angeles Times*, June 19, 1996.

58. Harrison, *Los Angeles Times*, June 19, 1996.

59. Harrison, *Los Angeles Times*, June 19, 1996.

60. Telephone interview with Marcia Bull, Attorney, Southern Poverty Law Center (November 8, 1996).

61. U.S. Commission on Civil Rights, *Transcripts of Community Forums, Burning of African-American Churches in (Alabama, Louisiana, Mississippi, North Carolina, South Carolina, and Tennessee) and Perceptions of Race Relations* (July 2–18, 1996); Jenkins interview.

62. Jerome interview.

63. Public Law 104–155.

64. National Fire Academy, *The National Arson Prevention Initiative* (Emmitsburg, Maryland: U.S. Fire Administration, 1996).

65. National Fire Academy.

66. Federal Bureau of Investigation, *Hate Crimes Statistics, 1993; Hate Crimes Statistics, 1994*.

67. National Asian Pacific American Legal Consortium, *Audit of Violence Against Asian Pacific Americans* (Washington, D.C., 1996).

68. Federal Bureau of Investigation, *Hate Crime Statistics, 1993; Hate Crime Statistics, 1994*.

69. Federal Bureau of Investigation, *Hate Crime Statistics, 1993; Hate Crime Statistics, 1994*.

70. Levin interview.

71. Levin interview; Morris Dees and James Corcoran, *Gathering Storm: The Story of America's Militia Network* (New York: Harper Collins, 1996), p. 112–122.

72. Levin interview.

73. Levin interview.

74. McDevitt interview.

75. McDevitt interview.

76. McDevitt interview.

77. David Johnston, "Hostility Toward Arabs and Jews Is Found on Rise," *New York Times*, February 7, 1991, p. A22.

78. Johnston, *New York Times*, February 7, 1991.

79. Untitled database text of a story about post-Oklahoma City tensions against Arab Americans, *Washington Post*, April 21, 1995.

80. Untitled, *Washington Post*, April 21, 1995.

81. Lieberman interview.

82. Levin interview; McDevitt interview.

83. Levin and McDevitt, p. 117.

84. McDevitt interview.

85. Levin interview.

86. Levin interview.

87. McDevitt interview.

88. McDevitt interview.

89. Levin interview.

90. Presentation by Kevin P. Giblin, unit chief, Terrorist Research and Analytical Center, U.S. Department of Justice, Federal Bureau of Investigation (National Research Council, Commission on Behavioral and Social Sciences and Education, Committee on Law and Justice, Planning Meeting, March 1996).

91. McDevitt interview.

92. Dees and Corcoran, p. 4.

93. Levin interview.

94. Levin interview.

95. Dees and Corcoran, p. 202.

96. Laurie Goodstein, ―Freemen's Theological Agenda," *Washington Post*, April 9, 1996, p. A3.

97. Dees and Corcoran, pp. 204-208.

98. Testimony of Mayor Emanuel Cleaver II, Kansas City, Missouri, before the Senate Committee on the Judiciary (March 19, 1996).

99. *State* v. *Stalder*, 630 So. 2d 1072 (Fla. 1994).

100. Anti-Defamation League, *Audit of Anti-Semitic Incidents, 1994* (New York, 1995).

101. The following jurisdictions criminalize interference with religious worship: California, Florida, Illinois, Indiana, Maryland, Massachusetts, Michigan, Minnesota, Mississippi, Missouri, Nevada, New Mexico, New York, North Carolina, Oklahoma, Rhode Island, South Carolina, South Dakota, Tennessee, Virginia, Washington, D.C., West Virginia.

102. ―Other" includes mental or physical disability or handicap (Alaska, California, Connecticut, Delaware, Illinois, Indiana, Maine, Minnesota, New Jersey, New York, Oklahoma, Vermont, Washington, Washington, D.C., Wisconsin), political affiliation (Indiana, West Virginia, Washington, D.C.), and age (Indiana, Vermont, and Washington, D.C.).

103. Other States have regulations mandating such training.

104. Rosemarie A. Miccacci, ―*Wisconsin* v. *Mitchell*: Punishable Conduct v. Protected Thought," *New England Journal on Criminal and Civil Confinement* 21(1995), p. 131.

105. 505 U.S. 377 (1992).

106. 113 S. Ct. 2194 (1993).

107. *See, e.g., Grover* v. *Florida*, 632 So. 2d 691 (Fla. Dist. Ct. App. 1994); *Florida* v. *Trabert*, 637 So. 2d 72 (Fla. Dist. Ct. App. 1994); *People* v. *MacKenzie*, 34 Cal. App. 4th 1256 (1995); *In re M.S.*, 896 P.2d 1365 (Cal. 1995); *People* v. *Aishman*, 896 P.2d 1387 (Cal. 1995); *State* v. *Vanatter*, 869 S.W.2d 754 (Mo. 1994); *State* v. *McKnight*, 511 N.W.2d 389 (Iowa 1994).

108. *See, e.g. Ayers* v. *State*, 645 A.2d 22 (Md. 1994), *cert. denied*, 115 S. Ct. 942 (1995); *State* v. *McKnight*, 511 N.W.2d 389 (Iowa 1994), *cert. denied*, 114 S. Ct. 2116 (1994); *State* v. *Mortimer*, 641 A.2d 2576 (N.J. 1994), *cert. denied*, 115 S. Ct. 440 (1994).

109. *Ayers* v. *State*, 645 A.2d 22 (Md. 1994), *cert. denied*, 115 S. Ct. 942 (1995).

110. *State* v. *Vanatter*, 869 S.W.2d 754 (Mo. 1994).

111. 65 F.3d 918 (11th Cir. 1995), *cert. denied* 116 S. Ct. 958 (1996).

112. 42 U.S.C. 3631 specifically provides that —whoever . . . by force or threat or force willfully injures, intimidates or interferes with, or attempts to injure, intimidate or interfere with—(a) any person because of his race, color, religion, sex, handicap . . ., familial status . . ., or national origin and because he is or has been . . . purchasing, [or] occupying . . . any dwelling . . . shall be fined under this subchapter or imprisoned not more than one year, or both. . . ."

113. *See also United States* v. *Lee*, 6 F.3d 1297 (8th Cir. 1993), *cert. denied* 114 S. Ct. 1550 (1994); *Cotton* v. *Duncan*, 1993 WL 473622 (N.D. Ill. 1993).

114. 656 So. 2d 479 (Fla. 1995).

115. William Branigan and John E. Yang, —House Passes Major Immigration Bill Without Reducing Legal Limits," *Washington Post*, March 22, 1996, p. A10.

116. Anti-Defamation League, *Audit of Anti-Semitic Incidents, 1994.*

117. Arent testimony.

118. Bishop and Slowikowski.

119. Lieberman, —Federal Action to Confront Hate Crimes."

120. Public Law 103-322, Title IV.

121. Public Law 103-322, Section 280003.

122. Arent testimony.

123. Community Relations Service, *Annual Report of the Community Relations Service* (Washington, D.C.: U.S. Department of Justice, 1995). This report was for fiscal year 1994.

124. Arent testimony.

125. Arent testimony.

126. According to the UCR, these States either did not participate in 1995, had fewer than 10 agencies submitting reports, or had fewer than 10 incidents reported: Alaska, Arkansas, Delaware, District of Columbia, Georgia, Hawaii, Illinois (excluding Chicago), Kentucky, Louisiana, Maine, Nebraska, Mississippi, Nevada, New Hampshire, New Mexico, North Carolina, Oklahoma, Rhode Island, South Dakota, Tennessee, Vermont, and Wyoming.

127. Part of the information in this chapter was gleaned from *350 Tested Strategies to Prevent Crime: A Resource for Municipal Agencies and Community Groups* (Washington, D.C.: The National Crime Prevention Council, 1996). Used with permission.

128. Leiberman interview.

129. Arent testimony.

130. Arent testimony.

131. Michael Lieberman, —The Hate Crime Statistics Act: The FBI's 1994 Report," *ADL Law Enforcement Bulletin* (New York: Anti-Defamation League, 1995), p. 1.

132. Arent testimony.

133. Levin and McDevitt, p. 231.

134. Levin and McDevitt, p. 239.

Bibliography

Anti-Defamation League. *Audit of Anti-Semitic Incidents, 1994.* New York. 1995.

Bishop, Eric and Slowikowski, Jeff. —Hate Crime." *Fact Sheet #29.* Washington, D.C.: Office of Juvenile Justice and Delinquency Prevention, U.S. Department of Justice. August 1995.

Branigan, William and Yang, John E. —House Passes Major Immigration Bill Without Reducing Legal Limits." *Washington Post*, March 22, 1996, p. A10.

Community Relations Service. *Annual Report of the Community Relations Service.* Washington, D.C.: U.S. Department of Justice. 1995.

Crumm, David. —Truth Emerges From a False Crisis." *Detroit Free Press*, September 3, 1996, p. A7.

Dees, Morris and Corcoran, James. *Gathering Storm: The Story of America's Militia Network.* New York: Harper Collins. 1996.

Fainberg, Anthony. —Terrorism and Hate Crimes in the U.S.: Prospects for the Nineties and Government Responses." Background paper for National Research Council, Commission on Behavioral and Social Sciences and Education, Committee on Law and Justice, March 1996.

Federal Bureau of Investigation. *Hate Crime Statistics, 1992.* Washington, D.C.: U.S. Department of Justice. 1993.

Federal Bureau of Investigation. *Hate Crime Statistics, 1993.* Washington, D.C.: U.S. Department of Justice. 1994.

Federal Bureau of Investigation. *Hate Crime Statistics, 1994.* Washington, D.C.: U.S. Department of Justice. 1995.

Federal Bureau of Investigation. *Hate Crime Statistics, 1995.* Washington, D.C.: U.S. Department of Justice. 1996.

Goodstein, Laurie. —Freemen's Theological Agenda." *Washington Post*, April 9, 1996, p. A3.

Hamm, Mark S. —Terrorism, Hate Crimes, and Anti-Government Violence: A Preliminary Review of the Research." Background paper for National Research Council, Commission on Behavioral and Social Sciences and Education, Committee on Law and Justice. March 1996.

Harrison, Eric. —Black Churches Have Long Been Targets." *Los Angeles Times*, June 15, 1996, p. A1.

Harrison, Eric. —Cristian Coalition Offers Blacks Repentance, Funds."
Los Angeles Times, June 19, 1996, p. A1.

Johnston, David. —Hostility Toward Arabs and Jews Is Found on Rise."
New York Times, February 7, 1991, p. A22.

Kapler, Robert. —Number of Hate Crimes by Blacks Rising, Rights Group
Says." *Justice Research*. Washington, D.C.: National Criminal Justice Association. November/December 1993. p. 3.

Klanwatch, a Project of the Southern Poverty Law Center. —The Dynamics
of Youth, Hate and Violence." *Klanwatch Intelligence Report*. Montgomery,
Alabama. October 1995.

Klanwatch, a Project of the Southern Poverty Law Center. *The Ku Klux
Klan: A History of Racism and Violence*. Montgomery, Alabama. 1991.

Labaton, Stephen. —Poor Cooperation Deflates FBI Report on Hate
Crimes." *New York Times*, January 6, 1993, p. A10.

Levin, Brian. —Bas Crimes: A Theoretical and Practical Overview."
Stanford Law and Policy Review (Winter 1993–94).

Levin, Jack and McDevitt, Jack. *Hate Crimes: The Rising Tide of Bigotry and
Bloodshed*. New York: Plenum Press. 1993.

Lieberman, Michael. —Federal Action to Confront Hate Crimes: Preventing
Violence and Improving Police Response." *New Challenges: The Civil Rights
Record of the Clinton Administration Mid-term*. Washington, D.C.: Citizens'
Commission on Civil Rights. 1995. p. 217-229.

Lieberman, Michael. —The Hate Crime Statistics Act: The FBI's 1994
Report." *ADL Law Enforcement Bulletin*. New York: Anti-Defamation
League. 1995.

Miccacci, Rosemarie A. —Wisconsin v. Mitchell: Punishable Conduct v.
Protected Thought." *New England Journal on Criminal and Civil Confinement*
21(1995), p. 131.

National Asian Pacific American Legal Consortium. *Audit of Violence
Against Asian Pacific Americans*. Washington, D.C. 1994.

National Asian Pacific American Legal Consortium. *Audit of Violence
Against Asian Pacific Americans*. Washington, D.C. 1996.

National Crime Prevention Council. *350 Tested Strategies To Prevent Crime:
A Resource for Municipal Agencies and Community Groups*. Washington, D.C.
1995.

National Fire Academy. *The National Arson Prevention Initiative*.
Emmitsburg, Maryland: U.S. Fire Administration. 1996.

NGLTF Policy Institute. *Anti-Gay and Lesbian Violence in 1994: National Trends, Analysis, and Incident Summaries.* Washington, D.C. 1995.

NGLTF Policy Institute. *Anti-Gay and Lesbian Violence, Victimization, and Defamation Report for 1991.* Washington, D.C. 1991.

NGLTF Policy Institute. *Anti-Gay and Lesbian Violence, Victimization, and Defamation Report for 1994.* Washington, D.C. 1994.

Office for Victims of Crime. *National Bias Crimes Training for Law Enforcement and Victim Assistance Professionals: A Guide for Training Instructors.* Washington, D.C.: U.S. Department of Justice. 1995.

U.S. Commission on Civil Rights. *Transcripts of Community Forums, Burning of African-American Churches in (Alabama, Louisiana, Mississippi, North Carolina, South Carolina, and Tennessee) and Perceptions of Race Relations.* July 2–18, 1996.

The World Almanac and Book of Facts. New York. 1996.

Sources for Further Information

Anti-Defamation League
823 United Nations Plaza
New York, NY 10017
Phone: 212–490–2525

Arab American Institute
918 16th Street NW., Suite 601
Washington, DC 20006
Phone: 202–429–9210
Fax: 202–429–9214

**Bureau of Justice Assistance
   Clearinghouse**
P.O. Box 6000
Rockville, MD 20849–6000
Phone: 1–800–688–4252
Fax: 301–579–5212
E-mail: askncjrs@ncjrs.org

Bureau of Justice Statistics
810 Seventh Street NW.
Washington, DC 20531
Phone: 202–307–0765
Fax: 202–307–5846

Community Relations Service
U.S. Department of Justice
600 E Street NW., Suite 2000
Washington, DC 20530
Phone: 202–305–2935
Fax: 202–305–3009

Disability Law Center
11 Beacon Street, Suite 925
Boston, MA 02108
Phone: 617–723–8455
Fax: 617–723–9125

**Facing History and Ourselves
   National Foundation**
16 Hurd Road
Brookline, MA 02146
Phone: 617–232–1595
Fax: 617–232–0281

Federal Bureau of Investigation
J. Edgar Hoover Building
10th and Pennsylvania Avenue NW.
Washington, DC 20535
Phone: 202–324–1143

Federal Bureau of Investigation
Criminal Justice Information Services
   Division
Attn: Uniform Crime Reports
1000 Custer Hollow Road
Clarksburg, WV 26306
Phone: 304–625–4995
Fax: 304–625–5394

Human Rights Campaign
1101 14th Street NW. , Suite 200
Washington, DC 20005
Phone: 202–628–4160
Fax: 202–347–5323

**International Association of Chiefs
   of Police**
515 North Washington Street
Alexandria, VA 22314–2357
Phone: 703–836–6767
Fax: 703–836–4543

**National Asian Pacific American Legal
   Consortium**
1140 Connecticut Avenue NW., Suite 1200
Washington, DC 20036
Phone: 202–296–2300
Fax: 202–296–2318

**The National Conference of Christians
   and Jews**
71 Fifth Avenue, Suite 1100
New York, NY 10003
Phone: 212–206–0006
Fax: 212–255–6177

National Congress of American Indians
2010 Massachusetts Avenue NW., Second Floor
Washington, DC 20036
Phone: 202–466–7767
Fax: 202–466–7797

National Council of La Raza
1111 19th Street NW.
Suite 1000
Washington, DC 20036
Phone: 202–785–1670
Fax: 202–776–1792

**National Criminal Justice
 Association**
444 North Capitol Street NW.
Suite 618
Washington, DC 20001
Phone: 202–624–1440
Fax: 202–508–3859

**National Gay and Lesbian
 Task Force**
2320 17th Street NW.
Washington, DC 20009–2702
Phone: 202–332–6483
Fax: 202–332–0207

**National Network of Violence
 Prevention**
55 Chapel Street
Newton, MA 02158
Phone: 617–969–7100
Fax: 617–244–3436

National Women's Law Center
11 Dupont Circle NW., Suite 800
Washington, DC 20036
Phone: 202–588–5180
Fax: 202–588–5185

**Office of Juvenile Justice and
 Delinquency Prevention**
810 Seventh Street NW.
Washington, DC 20531
Phone: 202–307–5911
Fax: 202–307–2093

Office for Victims of Crime
810 Seventh Street NW.
Washington, DC 20531
Phone: 202–307–5983
Fax: 202–514–6383

The President's Initiative on Race
The New Executive Office Building
Washington, DC 20503
Phone: 202–395–1010
Fax: 202–395–1020

Simon Wiesenthal Center
9760 West Pico Boulevard
Los Angeles, CA 90035
Phone: 310–553–9036
Fax: 310–553–8007

U.S. Commission on Civil Rights
624 Ninth Street NW.
Suite 700
Washington, DC 20425
Phone: 202–337–0382
Fax: 202–376–7558

U.S. Department of Education
600 Independence Avenue SW.
Washington, DC 20202
Phone: 202–205–5557
Fax: 202–205–5381

**U.S. Department of Housing
 and Urban Development**
451 Seventh Street NW.
Room 10000
Washington, DC 20531
Phone: 202–708–0417
Fax: 202–708–2476

Violence Against Women Office
950 Pennsylvania Avenue NW.
Room 5302
Washington, DC 20530
Phone: 202–616–8894
Fax: 202–307–3911

Women's Legal Defense Fund
1875 Connecticut Avenue NW.
Suite 710
Washington, DC 20009
Phone: 202–986–2600
Fax: 202–986–2539

Bureau of Justice Assistance Information

General Information

Callers may contact the U.S. Department of Justice Response Center for general information or specific needs, such as assistance in submitting grants applications and information on training. To contact the Response Center, call 1–800–421–6770 or write to 1100 Vermont Avenue NW., Washington, DC 20005.

Indepth Information

For more indepth information about BJA, its programs, and its funding opportunities, requesters can call the BJA Clearinghouse. The BJA Clearinghouse, a component of the National Criminal Justice Reference Service (NCJRS), shares BJA program information with state and local agencies and community groups across the country. Information specialists are available to provide reference and referral services, publication distribution, participation and support for conferences, and other networking and outreach activities. The Clearinghouse can be reached by:

r **Mail**
P.O. Box 6000
Rockville, MD 20849–6000

r **Visit**
2277 Research Boulevard
Rockville, MD 20850

r **Telephone**
1–800–688–4252
Monday through Friday
8:30 a.m. to 7 p.m.
eastern time

r **Fax**
301–519–5212

r **Fax on Demand**
1–800–688–4252

r **BJA Home Page**
www.ojp.usdoj.gov/BJA

r **NCJRS World Wide Web**
www.ncjrs.org

r **E-mail**
askncjrs@ncjrs.org

r **JUSTINFO Newsletter**
E-mail to listproc@ncjrs.org
Leave the subject line blank
In the body of the message,
type:
subscribe justinfo
[your name]